THE JOY OF BEING

JOBLESS

HOW TO OBTAIN

FINANCIAL FREEDOM

By

Taylore Vance

with

Herb Roi Richards

1673 S. Market Blvd. #143

Chehalis, WA 98532 (mailing Only) Tel. 360-748-4426

Cover design by Taylore Vance

Illustrations

    Hand drawn by Yolanda Eldora

    Computer graphics by Taylore Vance

    Cover by David M Masters

Copy Editor - Jim Alan

ISBN: 9798856566719

DEDICATION

This book (manual) is dedicated to the Law of Attraction.
The Law of Attraction has brought together all the
information that enabled me to find the right ingredients to
assemble these various ideas. It is a positive force in my life.
It never judges and always encourages. I owe all I have to it.
I appreciate its kind and firm hand, teaching and showing me
that I AM the creator of my reality.

If I could give you, the reader, only one gift, I would choose
to give you a better relationship with the Law of Attraction
and your inner self (the Life Manager).

The advice I would suggest is the lessons that I have learned:
- love who you are
- love what you are
- love where you are
- love what you have
- love where you've been
- all is a blessing

Before you try to move beyond.

with much love,
Taylore

PREFACE

Warning: This is not theory. As you read, you will learn how to constantly bring your dreams into physical reality. You will see how *what you are thinking, what you are saying, and what you are doing* affect your prosperity.

Your life is the result of your beliefs about it.

Destructive mind programs are similar to junk software in a computer-they clog and freeze up the thinking process. (Your stinking thinking is helping you create your life in a way you may not find pleasing.)

These patterns of recurring negative thoughts can be removed and replaced with positive affirmations and new knowledge (software for the mind) that encourage health and plenty-your birthright as a human being. For instance, "No pain-no gain" is a dogmatic expression and junk software for your mind. In fact, the more often you say or think it, the more painful it will be for you to get what you want.

Welcome to a journey into wealth and abundance.

These three actions – *thinking, saying, and doing* –have created your life as it is now. If you continue to do the same things you've always done, you'll continue to get the same results you've always gotten.

This manual will help you learn how to make small changes that will turn your life around and enable you to lead the life you have always wanted. It can be as simple as following a proven recipe for delicious chocolate cookies, and that is exactly what you get.

There is no need to make life hard. Lack of money missed chances, illness, sadness, limitations, frustration, and struggle are often caused by dogmas and old beliefs that you are still holding on to and they are not serving your best interests.

As you study this how-to manual, you will learn to release limitations such as the above dogma without going through a long, drawn-out ordeal. We also offer workshops where you get hands-on experience in this process.

Using the methods from either this manual or our workshops, or both, you can have these positive affirmations take effect immediately.

All that I am seeking is Now finding me.

Welcoming everything that happens to you-even the things you don't like-gives birth to new desires. New desires increase the flow of creative energy. That means feeling good more often! You will learn these things, and more, through the wisdom of Taylore and Roi's magical experiences and those of their students, who are walking this enchanted path to their own discovery of riches, whether they are physical or spiritual.

This is a do-it-yourself manual that shows you exactly how the natural laws of the universe work in regard to your gaining wealth in all areas of your life.

The system described has consistently brought an increase in prosperity of all kinds to all who practice it.

Most sages and masters agree that if you have poverty consciousness, you can kiss wealth goodbye!

You are in control of how much wealth you acquire, whether you are aware of this or not! It is more fun to be aware! You'll learn how you either push wealth away or attract it to flow abundantly into your life. It doesn't matter who you are-male or female, race, `place of origin, education, age, religion, or current outlook on life.

It doesn't matter how much money you have or don't have. It works even if you have only pocket change to your name, you've just been fired, the rent is due, the baby is sick, there is no food on the table, and your 1980 family car is not running. The seven principles work if you have thousands or millions of dollars. It doesn't matter if *all is well* or if *all is not well* in your life. You will see a great improvement in your life and finances as well as in other areas.

You will learn how to use natural laws in your favor.

Since you are attracted to reading this book, your inner knowingness has brought you here. It heard your frustration at a deep level, and it has brought you to find the keys to success. Your inner guidance system helps you to remember that you deserve abundance.

If you follow only one of the seven principles described in this book, you will experience an increase in wealth.

The unconscious thoughts that you send out are creating the life that you don't want. This is an education problem, and it can be solved right here and now. What is missing in your education is a way to *bridge the gap between poverty and plenty.*

So why isn't it happening like it should? (You need a burning desire —this question is a good start...)

Roi explains it well, "About ten years ago we discovered the power of words and word combinations in our lives. You can find a clue in the Bible, *First there was the Word...* [John 1] Sound is a very important component of any third-dimensional endeavor. Our spoken word defines our world and experiences. No matter where you are on the scale of wealth, regular and consistent use of these seven principles will increase your wealth in money, health, and well-being.

"We discovered two magic words that embody the spiritual Laws of the Universe. These words *bridge the gap."*

Here is a fact: Everyone in America has been taught poverty consciousness, except the very few wealthy people!

You will be taught how to use these words automatically so that your increase in wealth is an ongoing and continuous process.

The seven principles to creating your prosperity open the door to all kinds of prosperity: better health, relationships, friends, sex, and even more love, fun, joy, peace, happiness, fulfillment, satisfying work, and of course, financial wealth.

Taylore and Roi walk their talk.

Roi has been creatively jobless for most of his 94 years and Taylore joined him in joblessness nearly 44 years ago. This book explains why you may want to join the many thousands of jobless folks who live way above the average.

You will learn how simple it is to have the proper mindset to attract wealth without working for someone else and have **Fun** doing it.

Glossary

You want

You want wealth. Wanting brings more wanting-it can be an endless loop of frustration if the other steps aren't followed. This is the first step toward manifesting. Wanting creates desire, and desire creates passion. Passion is creative energy. Your wanting will lead you to find a way, a book, a successful person, etc. (The word want should not be used or written in your affirmations, because you'll get more want rather than your desired result.)

You believe

You have a belief that you can do it. A belief is made by thinking the same thought over and over. (Ican do it. I can do it.) This does not bring in your abundance, but it is the second step toward manifesting.

You know

When you know you can do it, it is yours. Knowing is the third step. Now all you have to do is follow a proven path, and the manifestation of your wealth is a done deal.

Abundance

There is much more available than you need in all areas of your life.

Remember that there is plenty to go around and that you are creating your abundance for the highest and best good of all concerned.

Constantly

Show that you know that a condition will be ongoing. Expect it. Expect this with your prosperity!

Cosmic Energetic Healing

Uses 7th dimensional energy and above. It uses advanced Laser Reiki techniques. It has been estimated that it is 100 times more efficient than other energy healing methods. It heals the energy body. When corrections are made to the energy body, physical body healing follows. CEH was also founded by Taylore and Roi.

Even more

This phrase can be used to show the universe that you already have some of (what you desire) and that you desire to have even more of it. This keeps you from coming from a place of lack. This phrase bridges the huge gap between poverty and plenty.

For the highest and best good for all concerned

In case casual thoughts begin to manifest, this allows   them to do no harm. It is good to say this phrase   often.

God – the Source of all

God is not some nasty dude in a white robe on a throne in the sky who'll get you if you don't be good. Not male or female, the Source is absolutely impartial and allowing. We are part of It – not separate! The seeming separation is   so we can enjoy our experiences individually. We are in the midst of It. We each are different aspects of It-Its bodies, minds, desires, etc.

We have Its experiences for It. The beauty of the plan is that no two experiences can be the same. And that's a good thing.

Imagination

A very important tool for bringing your desires into manifestation. Your ability to use mind images is how you create physical abundance.

In the process...

If you say, "I'm a millionaire!" then a part of your conscious mind will correct you by saying, "No, you're not!" That gets you nowhere. To bypass critical self-judgment you can say, "I'm *in the process* of becoming a millionaire!" Or, whatever you wish to become.

Junk Software

Just like in your computer your mind has conflicting programs. Consider where they might have come from. If you don't know it's true from your own experience, it's probably a glitch in your life operating behind the scenes and screwing up your joy and abundance. Example: "Don't talk to strangers!"

Often installed by parents when you were very young. Have they or anyone else uninstalled it? The mind must be regularly defragged like any other   computer.

Lack

Feelings of scarcity and being needy. Trying to get by. The underlying belief is that there's not enough to go around.

Feelings of lack cause a need for survival. They block your natural ability to flourish. If you come from a place of lack, you get more lack.

Laser Reiki

LR is Advanced Reiki and uses 6th dimensional energy and above to heal.

The nature & cause of problems are found by conversing with the subconscious mind. Emotional problems, chronic pain, and recurring patterns of lack and fear can be released and reprogrammed with LR. Taylore and Roi are the founders of Laser Reiki. You need no special tools or machines to do LR.

Law of Allowing

The third law. After you have done all the other things, you open your heart to receive. Next. be patient and wait expectantly.

Law of Attraction

The first law. Like attracts like. The simplicity of the universal laws escapes the understanding of scientists who thrive on complications.

Law of Focused Intent

When used with the above law, this will cause the universe to yield to your desire. Never give up on your dream. We suggest that you focus on peace and well-being for the Earth and its people, to help bring in a new paradigm of enlightenment.

The local branch of your subconscious mind where you can ask for help. It's multidimensional, works 24-7 and finds solutions to problems you present to it by your self-talk. It communicates with other subconscious minds to attract the right people, resources, methods, tools, techniques, ideas, procedures, money, strategies, and opportunities to help you.

Manifestation

This is the use of natural laws plus your imagination to bring forth abundance of all kinds. Consider manifesting as a game, and only practice it from a state of joy and love.

Always wish to bring forth the highest and best good for all concerned.

Money

Coupons representing stored God Source Energy. It's neither good nor bad. In the third dimension it is necessary so you can trade for stuff that brings you joy.

Our mission in life

Is to experience. You can't get it wrong; no mistakes are possible. No bad or good experiences happen. Some you'd like to repeat, some you'd rather not. They are all simply experiences for you and especially for the Source and fortunately no two are alike.

Prosperity

Everything in life is abundant for you-money, love, friendship, health, curiosity, contrast, etc.

Reiki

This age-old method of healing the body uses life   force energy through placement of the hands on or over the body. Uses 4-5th dimensional energy.

Security

This is an illusion that never lives up to its press. People make all kinds of compromises in pursuit of security. This is part of the lack mentality. It keeps you a prisoner in the box.

Self-talk

It is self-explanatory. But the key is to tune into your self-talk and see if it is benefiting you or if it's on a rerun of someone else's destructive and limiting self-talk. Clean up your self-talk and change your life.

Struggle

All the training that we receive from parents and schooling tries to prove to us that life is hard. You must struggle and work hard if you are to succeed. Struggle goes with the dogma: "No pain-no gain" and does not help you.

Subconscious

It's called the subconscious because your so-called conscious isn't aware of it.

Actually, it's not sub anything. A division of it called the Life Manager is the main controller of your life. Between them they control your whole show

Thank you, God

This phrase shows your gratitude for the behind-the-scenes activity that results in seemingly miraculous happenings. It is also very powerful when used in advance of receiving.

Understanding

Many people want to shortcut the system without the foundation of understanding. Take the time to completely read and study this manual at least twice.

Victim

One who feels powerless. One who feels his/her unliked experiences are caused by someone or something outside themselves. One who sends out victim vibration and doesn't realize it draws to them even more chances to be a victim.

What if _____ ?

A phrase that helps you use your imagination. It is an open phrase which leads to greater ideas and greater results. It avoids judgment.

Taylore Vance and Herb Roi Richards

CONTENTS

We suggest you build your own creative index as you read the text.

We did not index this manual. You are encouraged to create your own index, so you can easily find your personal points of interest.

When you find something, you want to return to put a mark at the edge of the page next to the item. On one of the blank pages in the back of the manual, write down the page number and a brief explanation.

Example:

We have found that the most important requirement for healing any negative pattern is first, finding the root cause.

Page 8-2   Root Cause

Roi

1

MY STORY: HOW WE LEARNED TO MANIFEST

WE CREATED THIS MAGNIFICENT LIFE - HERE'S HOW

I asked spirit to send me someone going my way.

My spouse and partner Roi and I have been teaching abundance, prosperity classes and energy healing workshops since 1994. I believe that our spirit guides are always working to get our attention and to help us expand who and what we are. Many times, they use money, like a carrot on a stick, to lead each of us to develop a more spiritual/holistic connection.

He had to be at least at my level spiritually or beyond.

There is an old dogma that says, "Money isn't spiritual." This is not true. Believing that saying could keep you poor if you are spiritual. And if you are rich, it could keep you from seeking a higher relationship with spirit. Some wealthy people are spiritually poor because they think money alone brings inner happiness. I believe those who seek a spiritual path will receive a bonus (financial prosperity) if they only allow it.

Roi showed up in less than two weeks.

When I met Roi, he was a motorcycle coach for racing and built high-performance automobile engines. He had sold his business a few years before.

We found that having a job is not a requirement for prosperity.

Roi and I have been living without jobs for many years, Roi since 1978, me since 1980. We got together in 1980 in San Antonio, Texas, while I was still employed by the US Army Mapping Agency at Fort Sam Houston. I quit my government job in the fall of 1980, and Roi and I left Texas for Idaho.

Anyone can have financial success if he follows some simple rules. This book contains hundreds of proven suggestions. Society tells you that to succeed you must work hard, have a good education, and find a job. But that is not the true path to wealth. We're showing you The Joy of Being Jobless without a job or lots of money. Does that sound good?

You create your own reality by your thoughts, beliefs, and actions.

After I left my government position, I thought about getting another job. Every time I applied for employment, things would come up, or someone else would get the job. I figured that I had other things to learn. I became self-employed sending out mail-order flyers, selling suppressed information on law and nutrition, and teaching courses. (Roi and I now have our own energy healing school near Chehalis, Washington. We'll tell you about it later.)

If you keep your dream in front of your mind, sooner or later it will become a reality.

We tried various methods of earning a living with small success in each different venture. We also lost most of our money in investments. Still, we always had a little money. We were never starving like the financial gurus described in the media. We never asked for handouts, unemployment benefits, or loans. We always followed our inner dream of being successful. We never gave up our dream despite how limited the outer world looked.

Remember, you are not alone. You each have guides and angels.

We came across a used book about prosperity at a yard sale: How to Solve All Your Money Problems by John Lester. We wanted extra copies for our friends, but it was out of print and not available in stores. That book put us back on track. We started thinking about our creation-our life. I already believed that, "You create your own reality by your thoughts, beliefs, and actions." That book brought our focus back to creating prosperity.

Angels and spirit guides have more time than we have because they are multidimensional.

We each have an inner guide, other guides, director, life manager, mahanta, spirit, angels, higher self, god, creator, etc., working with us. It doesn't matter what we call it. We all have some form of higher help standing by to guide us. I believe that Roi and I were spiritually led to find that book. It arrived for us as if on cue. Just as our manual, The Joy of Being Jobless arrived for you. Trust it's the perfect vehicle to help you right now.

They can work on your goals while you sleep!

Shortly after that, I was told about an offshore investment program where a person would receive 17% return per month. After watching it for several months, I finally put $10,000 into it. The very next month, it went sour. I went through several likewise investments. I don't give up easily! They were doing great until I invested, and then POW! They would go south.

I didn't let my "bad" investments get me down.

That made me dig deeper into how and why my investments were going so badly. It was as if I gave them the kiss of death. It had to be some kind of recurring negative program or pattern in my mind, not just bad luck. I don't believe in bad luck. I was unaware of consciously creating this challenge. I didn't know it at the time, but I had mental stumbling blocks on my road to prosperity. Losing money really made me think. It kept me wondering about the nature of the mind. I wondered, "Could negative thoughts shape the

4

outcome of my investments?" Yes! They could! Your inner climate creates your outer environment.

Sometimes it is best to just allow the death process to happen.

On the good side, if it weren't for those so-called bad investments, you wouldn't be studying this manual. There wouldn't be a prosperity manual. If I had given up, I would never have found the keys to prosperity, and I wouldn't be living the abundant life I am living now.

Back to my story... In 1985, I went to Arkansas to care for my ailing parents. My brother, who lives in Tennessee, was a CEO with the Monsanto Plant and couldn't take off like unemployed me. I was studying natural nutrition and thought I could help bring my parents back to life with raw food, colonics, and supplements. I soon discovered that they were racing to see who could get out of the physical world first. They had been together over 50 years, and neither one wanted to be left behind.

Despite how the outer world looks... all really is in Divine Order.

My mission with my parents turned into a spiritual one. I helped them pass from the physical world to the nonphysical. Mother left her body due to stomach cancer a little over two weeks after I arrived. Dad lasted three more months. His body died due to lung cancer, radiation over-treatment, a flu shot, and heart failure. I wasn't happy with my father's doctors. They over- cooked his already sick lungs with radiation and then nine months later insisted on a flu shot. He never recovered from the flu shot. I told the doctor, "I couldn't see how monkey pus (the flu shot) would help Mack," and it didn't. I was frustrated, that I couldn't help my folks with natural nutrition. After the doctors finished with their "practicing," there was nothing left to work on. Despite feeling helpless, frustrated and alone, I knew at a deep level that all was indeed in Divine Order.

We learned from Tony Robbins that fear is a powerful motivator, and you can use it.

Roi arrived from Idaho right after Dad left his body. Roi and I decided to stay in Little Rock and work on my parents' mobile home park. It had gotten run down, because they had been sick for the last few years. We repaired mobile homes for five years while we continued our studies in metaphysics and manifesting. Since we worked for ourselves, we had the time to both attend and teach seminars.

You can also turn fear into power.

We taught dream interpretation at the University of Arkansas. In bookstores, we taught spiritual enlightenment and soul travel. We did book reviews at metaphysical bookstores. In Houston, we worked on staff at Anthony Robbins' Fire Walk seminars. Robbins certified us in neurolinguistic programming (NLP). Robbins taught us many useful techniques. We found out that we can change reality from our studies with NLP.

Hundreds were flocking to the Robbins' fire walks. Why would anyone choose to walk on fire? The intention behind fire walks is to prove to you, beyond any doubt, that you have powers that fall outside the usual physical abilities. You are able to move beyond what you can consciously comprehend. Science and the real world are very different from what we are taught in school. Fire walking helps you to realize that it is necessary to think "outside the box." It also helps you to turn your fear into power, and to realize that fear is a no thing once you decide to go beyond it.

LISTEN TO YOUR INNER VOICE

When we had finished rebuilding the twelve mobile homes in Little Rock, Spirit pushed us to move on. An inner voice told me that our job there was finished. I was tired of trailer-park life, of renters waking me up in the middle of the night to call the police for them, etc.

In 1990, we left the trailer park in my brother's hands and moved to Washington State. We walked away with very little money and lots of stuff. The money had gone into repairing the trailers. Here's a list of the vehicles we had: a 1973 yellow Dodge van, a 1980 Nissan pickup truck that we had bought for $800 and fixed up, a flatbed trailer we borrowed, and a black Ford 250 truck we had bought at an auction and rebuilt the engine. We bought the Ford truck to pull the 5th wheel shop trailer we had bought and fixed up. The trailer had been used for a racing team and needed structural repairs and refinishing. The shop trailer contained Roi's tools and machines.

We needed a place to stay and to park our vehicles in Washington State. We placed small ads in the Little Nickel papers and found a 100-acre tree farm to rent where we could park the vehicles and live in a small spot in the center for practically nothing. We lived in the middle of the woods in our free double-wide mobile home with our two cats, Little Bit and Black. We paid only $24 a month for the rent, plus looked after the farm for the owner. We lived there for 10 years.

LEARNING TO MANIFEST ...

HOW WE FOUND A "FREE" MOBILE HOME

The fewer the unknowns, the easier the manifestation.

In manifesting, it helps to be familiar with the object of your desire. We had rebuilt mobile homes for five years and were comfortable with fixing them up. There were very few unknowns in this manifestation.

Fear of the unknown will keep you separate from your desired object.

If you want to bring your dream into reality ...get familiar with it. We manifested the double-wide mobile home for only $1. It was valued at the tax office for.

$24,000. Here's how we did it. We ran a small, classified ad in the Nickel paper. It stated: Retired couple wants a mobile home to fix-up. Must be reasonable. Have some cash. Write to POB _____ , Lacey 98503. We were living in the woods with no phone, and our mailbox was 35 miles away. Someone wanting to sell or give away a mobile home had to actually write a letter to us telling us what they had and how to get in touch with them. That's asking a lot of people these days. We received many replies. After several phone calls, we contacted the owner of the double wide. He had already offered it to a handyman who was moving it to Idaho. We were second in line. I decided that I would not worry about not receiving it. I told myself, "If it is meant to be, it will be ours. Otherwise, a much better one will show up!"

Who says you can't find an almost-free place to live?

Many people read our classified ad. We were offered several single-wide trailers and the one double-wide. After one long week, we received word: The double wide was ours, free and clear! Hooray!

We had never actually worked on a double-wide before. We had to figure out how it came apart and how to put its axles on. We arranged an appointment with a hauler. He offered valuable information on the teardown and setup, and on the paperwork and permits, etc., that were required to move it.

Spirit will usually give you a little more than you ask for.

We went to the Snohomish County seat to secure a release and found that the owner owed $324 in back taxes. We had to pay that before we were given the permit to move it. When we showed the owner what we paid, he quickly reimbursed us for the taxes. We celebrated this victory, too!

Remember to celebrate your victories because it increases your success.

He had lived in this mobile home while he built his new home. He really wanted it to be moved off his property as soon as possible. We had a few problems (learning experiences) in preparing it for transport and getting it out of the tight place where it was parked. Trees and bushes had grown up, water pipes had broken under the ground, sinking the mobile axle deep in mud, etc. The owner was actually afraid we'd give up. As the obstacles came up, we overcame them one by one. We were not giving up on our prize! We were winners!

So, you can get a sense of what it takes to manifest objects, here are some Important Steps we took. Try it yourself:

Assume it is already yours... The world is an abundant place. There is more than enough to go around!

1. Decide what you want.

2. Write what you want on a yellow pad or paper. You could make it like a letter with a list of things you choose.

3. Write out why you want this object.

   Dear Life Manager,
   *   I desire a better place to live because I have too much stuff. I'm tired of living in a 73 Dodge van. I think a mobile home would be good because we could park it on the rented land where we are now located. We know how to do this.*
   *   I am open to receive God's abundance. I am worthy of a better life. You are bringing us all this stuff (I'm very grateful*

10

for the many things you've brought, but I have no place to keep them, yet.)
    Thanking you in advance, I am your faithful coworker. (signed)
    Taylore Vance

4.   Find a place to put your object.

5.   Visualize what it might look like, always leaving room for spirit to make it even better or bigger.

A simple classified ad can be one of your steps to bring in your dream object.

6.   Make it real to your mind.   Become familiar with your goal.

7.   Know that your goal is possible.

8. List action steps for getting the process moving. Start immediately, acting on your first action step.

9. We wrote a small 3-line classified ad to announce what we were looking for. We placed the ad in papers, bulletin boards, etc.

10. Don't worry about the details. Let the universe fill it in, allowing your dream to be even   better.

I assumed that I was fully supported by the universe.

11. *Start celebrating* the accomplishment of your manifestation as if it were already finished. Tell yourself, "It's a done deal!"

12. Thank the "higher powers" for helping align you with your desired goal.

13. And finally, celebrate and express gratitude again, both when it was completed and on a continuous basis.

We manifested our mobile home with ease because we were familiar with them. The manifestation skids were greased.

Know that it is yours. There is plenty of what you want just waiting for you to claim it.

If we had asked for a million dollars, it probably wouldn't have been so easy. Why not? At that time, my energy field was not a vibrational match for a million dollars. My energy field would contain lots of unknowns, and maybe some fear about having a million dollars.

Your manifestation is easiest when you know your subject well. We knew about mobile homes. We had worked on them for 5 years.

If you don't know your subject well, you have some studies to do and/or you need to find a mentor who has walked the path before you-someone who can show you how it's done. If you are blazing a new trail for yourself, all kinds of internal fears may pop up, i.e., fear of success, fear of failure and fear to move forward. into the unknown.

Don't worry about it. Go have some fun while you wait.

At our energy healing school, we teach you how to release the root cause of these fears and other obstacles on your path to success. Please visit our Web site, www.CosmicEnergeticHealing.com, and learn more.

Once you know you deserve a million dollars, that manifestation will come, too.

I'm not saying that being able to manifest a million dollars is difficult. It is no harder than getting the universe to align you with a parking space when you go to town.

The difference is that you know you deserve a parking space. When the stakes get higher, all kinds of old fears come up and interfere with your abundance. I was a novice in manifestation when I manifested the mobile home. I figured that since Spirit wanted us to go west with no money, It had to support us by helping us get settled. I thought that I deserved a place to live.

USE VISUAL PROPS TO MAKE YOUR GOAL MORE REAL IN YOUR MIND!

I made a paper bracelet with hand drawn pictures of mobile homes colored with crayons. I put a lock of my hair on it and encased it in clear wrapping tape. I wore the mobile-home bracelet for several days. Even when I wasn't wearing it, the bracelet had a lock of my hair on it. Why do you think I did this? I wanted to imprint my energy field with a picture of my goal.

The more familiar you are with your desired goal, the easier it is to achieve.

Some people are pushing away their manifestation harder than they are pulling it into their lives.

Not only was I familiar with the idea of mobile homes, but also, I had made a statement by wearing the special bracelet. We were blessed with not only a free mobile- home but also an inexpensive storage trailer for our stuff, an authentic outhouse with the traditional crescent moon cut into the door, and the most beautiful home site setting in the middle of lush timber and pastureland in western Washington. The fact that we had no running water, had to use the outhouse and only had a wood stove was inconvenient. It was still a step up from living in the RV, and we felt blessed with the extra room.

New skills come easily when you ask for them.

We had the use of an antique bulldozer to cut a flat piece of land out between some huge evergreen trees. Both Roi and I took turns with the Cat, leveling the ground and pushing big rocks over the side of the grade. A month later, our new home was all set up. We moved from an old RV into the double wide. The next order of business was landscaping and building the organic garden. Roi will tell you about our great manifesting in that arena.

ROI FINDS THE BRIDGE WORDS

Roi: "Back in 1991, we'd just completed training in a mystery school where we were taught again that you couldn't get abundance from lack. I mulled this over in my mind for months. When you know that you don't have the money for the things you want, how can you possibly not come from lack? You can't lie to yourself, to the Source, or to the Life Manager (a division of the subconscious mind). The Life Manager actually runs your whole physical show. So job #1 is to convince it that you aren't coming from lack.

"I contemplated the Law of Attraction, which is as sure in its action as is the law of gravity. Like attracts like is another way to express it. In the Christian Bible that law is stated something like this: 'Whatever you sow is exactly what you reap.' Most people believe this only applies to your relationships with other people. I reasoned that it must apply to my relationship with myself, as well. Whatever I send out in thought comes back to me magnified. I noticed that if I thought, *I'm broke. I'd soon be clear out of money.*

Even if you have money, when you send out thoughts of being broke, the universe will make it true.

"Fortunately, Taylore never did think broke thoughts. Finally, the realization hit that I hadn't really been broke after all, because I'd had some money when I sent out those broke thoughts. Thinking that way, however, had insured that it would become true.

"My question then became, 'How could I think abundance thoughts without lying to the Universe?' Suddenly, after several months of contemplating this seemingly unsolvable problem, the answer came to me. I hadn't really been broke. I just could use even more of what I already had.

*The Bridge Words — **even more** — have proven themselves to work time after time.*

"You may think you are broke. But just look in your pockets or purse. I'm sure you'll find a little money. See? You already have some money. You're not broke. All you're after is even more. You are not coming from a place of lack.

If you come from a place of lack, you get more lack.

"In many ways we had abundance. I came up with the words even more abundance. For the next year, we said and thought that simple phrase every time we thought about money or anything else we wanted. During that year, we tripled our income without working any harder. Not only that, but we were given an abundance of used pallets to put around our fruit trees to keep the deer from eating them, dozens of 5-gallon buckets, cedar boards to build the raised beds in our organic garden, building materials, etc. Later, we got tired of turning down stuff that was offered to us, so we changed the wording of our mantra. We changed it to these words that we now use to bridge the gap between poverty and plenty -- *"Thank you, God, for constantly bringing us even more money!"*

By now, we hope that you understand that all wealth or poverty happens in the mind first, and then it shows up in your physical circumstances. It doesn't matter whether you are educated, male or female, or tall or short. The color of your skin and where you live don't matter. The Law of Attraction works the same for everyone, 24 hours a day, seven days a week, whether you use it to your advantage or disadvantage.

You, too, can have even more. Make it a habit to look for an increase of money.

Thank you, Roi, for sharing "even more."

Most other authors of books about creating prosperity and wealth started out with some affluence and then created lots more. Almost all of them had some type of regular job or employment, too. We didn't have much money. And we didn't have jobs.

Now it's your turn to make a commitment and to set your focused intent on your goal.

We have proven that you can start immediately from where you are-regardless of whether you have a job or no job. You can start right now with what you have. You will increase your income by at least 300% by following the simple steps above and studying this manual until you fully understand why these principles work. You are in the business of reprogramming your conscious mind to accept abundance. Once you do that, the Life Manager will help you fulfill your dreams.

You are learning to do this!

Hundreds like yourself have already increased their income using these simple techniques. Now it's your turn!

NOTES:

2

USING THE LAW OF ATTRACTION

THE UNIVERSE HELPS YOU

Even if you didn't know about the Law of Attraction, it still works in all areas of your life. Your senseless mind chatter is as much an order to the Universe as are the bridge words you are learning to use. Why settle for a haphazard, low-quality life when you can program in as much order and abundance as you can stand?

The Universe rearranges itself to accommodate your picture of reality.

I'll start right off by giving you the so-called **magic words** we found that *bridge the gap between poverty and plenty!* They are as follows:

"EVEN MORE"

"Thank you, Source, for constantly providing me (or us) with even more money."

Using that phrase will get you wealth. It doesn't matter whether you start with a penny or thousands of dollars. It is

19

important not to come from lack. So, you must agree that you already have some of what you want more of and it can be anything.

A good example of the power of these two words happens every time we share them. Roi and I teach a one-day seminar called Creating Your Prosperity. In May 2002, Rev. Brown of the Centralia Unity Church, WA, interviewed us at his office to see if our 1 Day prosperity program would be suitable for his church members. We gave him a brief preview outlining what we teach. It must have taken 45 minutes total for him to review the fill-in-the-blank manual and listen to a very abbreviated program. Six months later when the date came for us to present to his congregation, he had quite an impressive personal success story to share with the class. He'd put into practice a few simple exercises we'd shown him using the words even more!

How are you going to take care of the object of your manifestation?

What details need to be taken care of before the universe will take you seriously?

The result was the best 4th quarter in 23 years as an architectural designer, even with the economy down. Through the use of the prosperity exercises, he overcame what was going on around him to prosper in his business. As of today, he still uses these words every day.

In order to manifest, decide what you want, write it down or find a picture of it.

Another important point is that the Universe (via the Life Manager) uses other people as its conduit for wealth. You are thanking the Life Manager and the Universe in advance, and you know these blessings yet to come are already on their way. You will be receiving its products via other people. So, you will realize affluence much more quickly if you put yourself out there where other people are and interact with them in some way.

The Universe uses other people as its conduit for wealth.

Using the Law of Attraction:

1.   It starts with your desire for a better life.

2.   You must work through your feelings about whether you deserve a better life or not.

3.   You must know that it is possible for you since others have done it.

4.   Make up your wish list by writing it down and editing it until it reads exactly the way you want it. This working and reworking of your wish list makes it more real to your conscious mind while defining the dreams and expanding on the details aligns it for action with your subconscious mind.

5.   Get out and take action. You can't sit on the couch eating chips and watching TV and expect the Life

Manager to come and place what you want in your lap. You need to get out and stir around.

When you work smart, you have engaged the whole universe in working with you in a positive manner.

6. Find someone you can model if possible. "If one of us can do it... then any of us can, too!" That is a good point of view. It helps the conscious mind accept even more wealth.

7. See your life changing into the picture you desire. Visualize it as a done deal. Spend 5 minutes doing this.

8. Have some passion about your new life. If you don't feel passionate about your new life- start acting as if you do. Fake it until you make it.

9. Began writing a detailed letter to the Life Manager stating why you want this wonderful life and asking it to line up the necessary experts in the form of people, methods, technologies, tools, and money to help you succeed. Always leave room for the Life Manager to make it even better for you!

10. Once you get the wealth ball started rolling your way, even if it's a little trickle or wealth, continually using "even more" in all of your thoughts about abundance keeps the wealth ball rolling.

11. After we discovered "even more" our tiny business started getting too many checks, so we changed our saying to "even more spendable cash money." The business continued to expand with very few checks.

12. Show gratitude; Thank you Source, God, etc. for helping me understand that you have already taken care of _____ _____ _____ even beyond my wildest dreams. Thank you, thank you, thank you.

From personal experience, we found that one of the most important ways to create true prosperity is to clear away the negative programming from our minds.   Prosperity first happens between your ears. Prosperity, or the lack of it, is in your mind and your thoughts. Your thoughts and expectations either limit or expand your prosperity. Abundance is all around you, trying to find its way to you. You just have to open up and claim it.

Law of Attraction

Life is good
All is in Divine Order

I always have Plenty of Money

No matter what happens it always turns out for good

All is well

Money comes to me easily

People are always handing me money!

I embrace love, joy, peace, fun, freedom, expansion and abundance

The Law of Attraction mirrors back to you Exactly what you send out

Law of Attraction

Life is hard
It is unfair
I'm sick and tired
of it

Poor me,
I owe, I owe
off to
work I go

No matter
what
happens
it always
turns out
bad for me

I can never
get ahead

Everybody
is out
to get me!

You
have to
work
hard

It's a tough world
out there. The harder I
work the behinder I get.

The Law of Attraction <u>DOES NOT JUDGE</u> what you send out. It just mirrors it back.

WORKING SMART

Most of our mental and emotional programming comes from outside ourselves -- childhood, school, books, all kinds of media, teachers, and friends and family are all geared into making us believe that we have to work hard to have success. Life doesn't have to be hard. Roi and I made it without working any harder than we were working when we were poor. You can, too. Working smart is more fun than working hard.

If hard work made you rich, then ditch diggers would be millionaires.

Once you learn to clear the mental stumbling blocks, you will see how the Universe rearranges itself to accommodate your picture of reality. It is already doing that. It is accommodating your picture of a limited reality -- otherwise you wouldn't be studying this manual.

Trust that your supply is the Source (God), and its vehicles are the people. The Source is unlimited, and its supply is everlasting.

Imagine what will happen when you are able to expand your picture of reality in a positive manner.

That's what happened to us. We expanded our picture of reality, and our life together changed for the better. Roi and I were poor, but we had dreams. We manifested a beautiful place to live in the middle of 100 acres plus many free amenities. We built trails for hiking and motorcycle riding.

Once we were settled in, we took $500 and started a weekend business buying and selling items at sport expositions, flea markets, gun shows, etc. This weekend work gave us operating money with a very low overhead.

Only your lack of preparation and allowing can keep it from you.

PICTURES ON THE REFRIGERATOR DOOR

What does manifesting mean? It means bringing one of your dreams forward into physical reality.

Here in the physical (third dimension) this usually takes place over a period of time and involves the actions of several people.

It helps not to worry and not be tied to a specific outcome, because what shows up could be even better than you could have possibly imagined.

We wondered what it would be like to have a small tractor for working in our yard and garden. Roi and I saw a display of farm equipment at the Southwestern Washington Fairgrounds some years ago. We looked over the tractors very carefully. I picked up a flyer on the small, 12-horsepower Kubota. Upon arriving home, I took scissors and trimmed out a small photograph of the tractor. It had both a front loader and a backhoe. I taped the photo to the refrigerator door and made the statement to the Universe, "This is what I want! Thank you, God!"

This tractor would have cost $26,500 new. Once in a while, we would look for one in the classified ads, but even used, they were still too expensive. Remember we were living in the woods and still did not have a lot of money. A couple of our friends have Kubota tractors. We always admired the versatility of these tractors. We noticed how well they worked for their small size. All we needed to do was find one that fit our budget.

Practice the Law of Allowing. Open your heart to receiving and allow the object of your desire to move into your space.

We were teaching classes and helping other people manifest even more prosperity in their lives. Four years passed, and we still didn't have our tractor. We had already manifested outright quite a few other things.

Once you take worry out of the situation, your object of desire is freed up to move toward you. Worry and fear are blocks to being able to receive. They close you up. They actually push your desired target away from you.

Worry and unease of any kind about it will keep it away from you.

The photo of the Kubota was still on the refrigerator door. Four years and no tractor! This made us wonder if we were following our own advice. I asked the Life Manager and my angels, "What is missing? Why don't we have the tractor?" Within a few days, we heard about a neighbor who was moving out of the area. He had a garage he wanted to give away. We thought this would give us a shed where we might park the Kubota. We took him up on his free offer. We disassembled the garage, hauled it home, and reconstructed it. Now we had a home for the dream tractor.

Celebrate! It helps to celebrate when you are manifesting... because the angels then know that they are helping your moving in the right direction.

One week after we built the tractor shed, we were in a meeting and Roi "happened" to sit next to a man who owns a local Kubota agency. He just "happened" to receive a used Kubota with front loader and back-hoe on consignment earlier that day. It was just what we were looking for and at the right price. It couldn't have been a better match! We now have the tractor we wanted, and at a reasonable price. Yeah! Celebrate! And express gratitude!

The angels have tremendous power but little understanding of the third dimension.

Less than two weeks after we built the shed, we had the tractor parked under it. Our dream Kubota tractor finally came home to roost.

How did the tractor get off the refrigerator door and into our hands? After four years, what made the difference? What was the turning point? Was it the shed we built where we could park it? Were we then complete and ready to receive? Anything that gives you an uneasy feeling about receiving your manifestation slows its arrival or holds it just outside your reach. Examine your gut feelings about your desire. Are you fully in alignment with receiving? Have you built your shed?

Act as if the object of your desire is already present.

Remember the movie *Field of Dreams,* where these famous words were spoken, *"Build it and they will come. "?* This is a good example. You must do the groundwork and make a place where your manifestation can arrive. If you want a million dollars, then make business plans. Where will you store it? How will you spend it? Being ready will facilitate the flow of energy toward the desired goal. And remember to have even more fun and celebration along life's journey.

It's the journey, not the destination, that's important.

ABUNDANCE THROUGH REIKI

Are you having fun yet? If not, then you're not doing it right!

In 1985 while living in Arkansas, we had learned Reiki I and II. Reiki is an ancient hands-on-healing procedure for the body, mind, and spirit. You learn how to flow Universal love energy. You are not using your own energy, so flowing it never tires you out. You can flow it to yourself and to others.

Ask and you shall receive.

In 1991 a couple of years after moving to Washington, I took a weekend course in Reiki III, the master level. As soon as I returned home, I attuned Roi to the Reiki III energy current, so that he could also enjoy the new level of connection to Source energy. I think that everything should pay for itself, so I began to teach Reiki at the local metaphysical bookstore in Chehalis, WA. After several classes, I had recouped the cost of my Reiki master training.

Magic words bring magic into your life.

We desired more magic in our lives. We were led to discovering more magic words that felt good to say.

After a few months of being Reiki masters, Roi and I began to ask Spirit if there was more to healing than just traditional Reiki. I was getting a little bored spending 1 to 1 ½ hours applying a Reiki treatment to just one person. Spirit answered with a question, "Taylore, how would you like to be able to heal 10 people at the same time you are now healing one person with Reiki?" "Oh, wow!" I thought, then I added, "I'm all ears." With time speeding up, earth moving into the 4th dimension, I was ready to move into a much higher gear. Information about energy healing flooded into my life – both inner and outer.

In 1994, Laser Reiki and Cosmic Energetic Healing were created; these energy healing techniques just sort of grew out of our desire to help others. These methods healed ten times faster than traditional Reiki or other energy healing methods we know. We started another weekend business teaching energy healing workshops all over the country. In 2000, Spirit told me that we needed to have a retreat center where we lived, but the owner of the property we had rented for 10 years didn't want groups of strangers on his land. I was a little disappointed. Conflict causes you to seek another way. Conflict is good-it makes you think about things you haven't learned about yet. Out of confusion and chaos comes order.

The words, "Even more love, joy, freedom, expansion, well-being, health, abundance, and prosperity. Thank you, God" brought magic to us.

LOVE WHERE YOU ARE

Before you think about moving to a new place or job, you'd better find some joy about where you are. Otherwise, you will re-create a new place with the same limitations you now have. Focus on the problems where you are, and you'll get more problems in the next place or job.

This is a fact. These magic words we were using were activating a whole new level of prosperity for us.

Where we were living was a great place. We were renting a couple of acres in the middle of the woods. Outside the 100 acres there were other forest lands. We were never bothered by neighbors. We had none. Our organic garden was the best. It grew huge vegetables in abundance. We had worked on the soil until it was perfect. We could ride our motorcycles in the woods and trails for twenty miles, starting right from our own doorstep. We could fish in the Chehalis River where it crossed the lower end of the property. There were two spring-fed trout ponds near the mobile home. We could hunt deer and bear in the yard if we wanted. Roi decided that the deer weren't lost and didn't need hunting. We respect nature and wildlife. We like to think of our place as a sanctuary for wildlife.

Still, with all this abundance, we wanted even more. We wanted a place to live where we could invite students to come to workshops and retreats.

Always create from a place of joy and love.
Otherwise, you won't like your new creation.

How could you use this method in your life? Say you want a new house or a better job. If you hate the job, you have now, you resent spending all your time working there, or the salary or people there smell bad, then you have a good chance of re-creating the same circumstances in a new job.

Many people will hate what they are doing, hate where they are living, and expect the Universe to give them a better life. It doesn't work that way if you want to manifest a better life, we believe it is better to find a way to notice all the benefits. Otherwise, you keep manifesting the same old stuff over and over.

So, in order for us to manifest a better place to live, we made a special effort to acknowledge the benefits of where we were living.

When you are manifesting from a place of joy
and appreciation, the results give you the fun in
life that you've been longing for.

We embraced loving where we were while we entertained thoughts of, *"Even more love, joy, freedom, expansion, well-being, health, abundance, and prosperity. Thank you, God. "*

I took pictures of the new place we had found.

Soon a realtor friend let us know of a nearby property that was for sale. We looked at it. It had a two-story building right next to the main house that was perfect for the energy healing school. It had a large shop and several outbuildings for Roi's automotive tools and motorcycles   left over from a collection he had back when. The two-story house, which you can see in the photos, was perfect-large enough for the two of us and all the students who wanted to bunk in for the retreats. Sometimes we have 15 to 20 students here, and our classes are growing all the time.

I put some photos on the refrigerator door.

How did we get the house? We have no jobs. We have no credit. After our investments went sour, we had no large cash reserves. At the time, I had no idea how this place was going to be ours. I just went with what worked in the past – pictures on the fridge and knowing we could take care of such a place.

WORDS THAT CREATE DREAMS

As I looked at the beautiful photos of the dream property, I said, *"Thank you, God, for even more love, joy, freedom, expansion, well-being, health, abundance, and prosperity. Thank you for helping me understand that You have already taken care of securing this property for us even beyond my wildest dreams."*

We blessed our water with these words and drank it. We blessed our food with these words and ate the food.

All that was left was to relax and put our attention on loving where we were. (This step is very important.)

We made an offer on the property. The landowner wanted to meet us. We met him and our friend the Realtor, Rebecca. She told us that other people were interested in buying the property. We arranged for the owner to show us the land. That means walking all over the 22 acres. We looked at the spring, which was off the property in the woods behind. We looked at the spring- fed mountain stream near the main house, pond, new trees planted, hot tub, garden area, and all the buildings.

All is well. All is in divine order.

It had no well, only spring water piped in from half a mile away to a collection tank and piped into a practically new pump house with a sanitation system for the water. We spent almost all day with him while his wife hung out with Rebecca in the house. He came down $20,000 and made a counteroffer. He liked us. We increased our next offer by only $1000. He came down again and it was accepted. He carried the note, and at closing there was exactly enough money, to the penny, to cover everything including the unexpected expense of homeowner's insurance that was due before we could close. I had thought we could buy that later. The title company personnel were amazed that the escrow money was exactly correct to the very last penny! I think that was Spirit showing me that all was in Divine Order.

When you want a better home or a better job, remember that you will continue to get what you are focusing on. So when you hate your current job and desire to be over there in a better job, on one hand you have desire, and that is good. Desire causes you to flow creative energy.

On the other hand, when you dislike your current job, you are sending out a powerful, invisible energy field of hostility. Feelings of *dislike or hate* to cause the creative energy to *give you more of that same frequency.* As long as you dislike where you are, it is difficult to move into a better position. You might change jobs, but the new job will turn into a situation just like the old one.

Frequencies you send out will attract matching frequencies.

Good or bad – it matters not.

What you send out in your thinking returns to you magnified. Send out how much you hate where you are, and you'll end up where you hate it even more.

SEE WHAT A POWERFUL CREATOR YOU ARE

The way around this dilemma is to start cataloging and focusing on all the nice stuff about that job. Maybe you met someone special as a result of being at that job? Find something good you can focus on. Focusing on good brings good!

BE OPEN TO RECEIVE THE ABUNDANCE

Visualize that you are supported by the Universe. See all your needs being met.

Appreciate the great attributes of where you are, and you will receive even more wondrous surprises in your manifestations. Use the unstoppable power of the Law of Attraction to continuously live the abundant life you've always desired.

Feel the support! (You already are deserving of support from the Universe!)

You can affirm: *There is a wonderful new job waiting for me. This company is looking for exactly the same type of person I am. I have the skills they need. The boss will be delighted with my dedication to details. Other kind and loving people will also be employed there, and they will love and respect me. They will pay me a good salary. I am worthy, I am good enough, and I deserve a great job and a great salary! Thank you, God, for this opportunity!*

A list for the Universe is a necessary tool for putting the Law of Attraction to work for you.

*If we have invisible helpers then you, too, have
invisible helpers.
Use them! (We are not alone!)*

Now is the greatest time to choose your thoughts and
make your list for the Universe to complete. Yes, I really
mean you have invisible help to work on your list if you
allow it to do so. Now, why not ask for what you really want?
(We don't mean "asking" like begging but stating a fact as if
it's a done deal!) You are time traveling into the future and
looking at your dream or goal as if it already has been
accomplished.

*Look at your dream with gratitude in your heart,
seeing it already finished.*

The Life Manager loves you to be in gratitude. Roi and I'd
like to share these words with you: *"Thank you (Life Manager)
(Source) (God) (Creator) (Universe) for helping me understand that
you've already taken care of (each individual item on my list) even
beyond my wildest dreams."* Note: Name the things on your
list individually.

THE POWER OF MAKING LISTS

One of the greatest magic tricks to living an abundant life
is the power of making lists. I have made many lists. I make
them and forget about them. Years later, I'm moving, and I
find an old list. Every time this happens, I'm amazed. All the
items on the list have been accomplished, seemingly without
effort.

The Life Manager is working on my list while I sleep, while I work in the garden, while I play, while I go to a movie, etc. How else would it know what to do? It needs your list so it can help you. The list of things that you want the Universe to complete is one of the magic tricks that ensures success.

It is necessary to make a list of what you expect from the Life Manager for a couple of reasons. First, it helps you to think clearly about your desires without sprinkling your thoughts with negatives. Second, on a list the essence of your desire can be clearly stated.

We manifested many, many things by… not coming from lack.

I've worked with clients who did not know what they wanted out of life. They started by making lists of what they did not want. One young client finally decided that he didn't want to be broke, was tired of being lonely, and was not happy with the direction his life was going. He took his pen and paper and wrote down the things that he didn't want. Then I showed him how to turn the negative statements around. He then wrote, "I want money, I want a girlfriend, and I would like some direction in my life." I told him, "That's much better. But now you have to rewrite it coming from a place of completion, not lack."

The subconscious mind, working with the universe, will give you anything — even some things you don't want.

Working

WORKING WITH THE SUBCONSCIOUS MIND: IF YOU COME FROM LACK, YOU GET MORE LACK

If you want money, what are you going to get? The *want* of money.

So, you need to pretend you already have some money. You have a little bit of money in your pockets, right? When you have some money, you are not coming from lack. So, you will not get more of the lack. Okay! You have some money and could use <u>even more</u> money. Now what are you going to get? Even more money! See how a play on words can take you from lack and put you into a receiving position?

Now the young man's list looked like this: I have some money and could use even more money, even more girlfriends, and even more direction in life. About the girl friend-he probably can remember a time when he had one. Otherwise, I'm sure he can get a date. There are lots of lonely people just wanting to be asked to join you for a cup of tea. He may need to feel self-worthy and good enough about himself to be able to ask for a date. Lack of self-esteem keeps people down and keeps them from asking for the very thing they want.

Lack of self-esteem not only keeps you down, it also keeps your abundance away.

The words even more are bridge words that help you come from substance, instead of coming from lack.

If you come from lack of joy,
you will get more lack of joy.

Writing down a list of positive things that you desire to have in your life forces you to focus your attention. Now you can begin to get what you want, instead of continuing to get what you don't want. You can write anything in the world on your list. No one judges your list. The Life Manager already knows your deepest desires and will give them to you when you ask in the correct manner. This is your life. It is not a dress rehearsal or some stage play. It is the real play called "your life." You are more in control of your life than you think.

You are not alone, because you have the Life
Manager and higher forces always with you,
working to make your dreams come true.

The forces that are don't really care or judge you. You can put anything on your list. Even while you sleep, you have help from the forces that are at work on your list. These invisible forces need you to make the list, so they know the direction to go with your life. You'd be surprised at the helpers that are just waiting for you to make your list.

Your greatest power is your ability to choose how you feel and what goes on your wish list. You may have forgotten that you also have the ability to choose many things about your life. You have the right to choose your friends, choose your emotions, choose what you'll put up with, and what you'll not put up with. You're not stuck in a dead-end job, in an undesirable place to live, or in a relationship that is not benefitting you. Your right to choose is an awesome inner power and those decisions will instantly change your outer world. I'm constantly making choices about my life and adding to the wish lists I give to the Life Manager.

I suggest that you write your goals on your list like affirmations.

Your desire can be stated like a done deal. You see it as a finished project and feel the gratitude of accomplishment. Admire the dream. "When you pray a prayer of thanksgiving for all the blessings *yet to come,* you are doing something *very powerful."* (From Neale Donald Walsch's newsletter.) His first book was *Conversations with God.* He has several great books to help you see your relationship to God, or whatever you choose to call the Source of all there is.

Thankfulness will always bring you even more things to be thankful for.

One of the laws of the Universe is that you receive back what you send out, magnified. This law works whether or not you are aware of it, believe it, or disbelieve it. It works just as well when you send out negative thoughts and sayings, such as "poor me," "nothing ever goes right," "I can't do that," "no pain -- no gain," "I'm always broke." The law sees no difference between those negative thoughts and, "Thank you, God, for bringing me even more spendable cash money." It simply brings you what your self-talk demonstrates that you desire.

"Your wish is my command," says the Life Manager.

The Universe is pliable, and it can and will rearrange the world to fit your picture of how you see your life.

Notice what thoughts you are thinking. Like I said, one of your greatest powers is to choose your thoughts. Are they mostly beneficial? Are some of your thoughts mind chatter, automatic responses, and other useless "put-me- downs"?

You must give the Life Manager some input. Give it a program or a wish so it will work for you. It is now time to write your personal list of things for the Universe to complete while you go about your life.

Check the different areas of your life that could use improvement with an **X**. List other areas that are particular to your lifestyle.

Family
    Children
    Parents
    Spouse

Job

Business

Investments – Residual Income

Retirement plans

Recreation
    Vacations, trips, movies, concerts, baseball games, races, etc.
    Boats, homes, equipment, RVs, motorcycles, airplanes
    Things you want to learn how to do: skiing, bike riding, snowboarding, tennis, etc.

Home

Cars

Projects to do or to build

Education – For yourself, spouse, children

Write your list! Then thank God or the Source of all life for the completion of all the items and projects on the list - as if they were already accomplished. Take a deep breath and let go of all the struggle that you used to associate with writing lists. Know that it is a done deal!

List for the Universe:

(I am ready to receive even more of . . .)

Things I'd like to do or learn how to do:
                (Don't forget to play more!)
1. Learn the Laser Reiki training
2. Become the master I was always meant to be
3. Learn muscle testing to communicate with the life manager
4.
5.
6.
7.
8.
9.
10.

Things I would like to have or own:
(Somewhere on the timeline I have already claimed these things.)

1.
2.
3.
4.
5.
6.
7.
8.
9.
10.

Today I will accomplish: (put only 3 items here knowing that the Universe is working full time on everything). Feel the gratitude!

1.

2.

3.

I'd like to see this accomplished:
(Improvements on a large scale, perhaps for the whole world)
1.
2.
3.
4.
5.
6.
7.
8.

Things I would like to be:
(Suggestion -- Think some really big thoughts, too!)
1.
2.
3.
4.
5.
6.
7.
8.
9.

MAKE IT SO!

Thanks to Abraham Hicks for this wonderful idea of a list! It helps you get your mind straight and it makes it clear what your current dreams are.

We added these three items to their list: feelings of gratitude, thank you, God or Source, and release of struggle.

All really is in Divine Order! Lists are fun! They line up universal energy. You are allowing the Universe to work on your list 24-7.

I could always use even more of:

1. Love, joy, health, well-being, peace, and harmony in my life. Fun, healing, rejuvenation, regeneration of my body, giving me radiant heath, stamina, and vitality.

2. Abundance, prosperity, money, good opportunities, success, friends, support for my projects, students for my school, clients, completion of the things I've started, etc.

3. Adventure, travel, new car, new home, friends, time to play, finish my book, go fishing, hiking, bike riding, horseback riding, gardening, etc.

What could you use even more of:

1.

2.

3.

4.

5.

6.

7.

8.

9.

3

INVISIBLE CAUSES OF FAILURE

HOW TO TURN YOUR LIFE INTO A SUCCESS!

You can do all the right things in setting up your business or your life and still be unhappy. There are **invisible forces** behind the scenes that affect your actions and may sabotage your best efforts with friends, lovers, bosses, customers, suppliers, or bankers. They affect both your business and job, and your relationships and personal life. The stage for success or failure is set first in the mind, then plays out in what we call real-life drama.

Some people have an instinctive understanding of how this all works, and everything comes easily for them.

Have you ever wondered why some people seem to have it easier than you do? Do you think they are lucky? What is success based on? How hard you work? Your education? Who you know? Being in the right place ·at the right time? What you think about yourself? Your expectations? Do you feel like you're good enough? Do you fear being successful? Do you fear failure? Do you fear responsibility, or that you'll let someone down?

SELF-SABOTAGE IS VERY SUBTLE

Internal level self-sabotage affects physical-level outcomes. Most people are unaware of the *behind-the-scenes activity* in their minds that can push success away from them. Some people have an instinctive understanding of how this works, and everything comes easily for them. Others have varying degrees of understanding and may be completely unaware of these forces. You can learn to control these activities and forces.

Health and well-being are natural to you.

When you are in disharmony with things sickness and illness is possible. Work to be in harmony.

The symptoms of self-sabotaging beliefs are *stress, anxiety, frustration, worry, anger, and lack of energy.* Self-sabotaging beliefs keep energy blockages in place in the body. These blockages lead to lack of health and well-being in all areas of your life, including your finances. Once these self-sabotaging beliefs are removed, the flow of healing energy is increased. Health and well- being are natural to the body. Natural abundance (including plenty of money) is a major part of our birthright and is available to all humankind. When you have great success, no one else is deprived of anything. Shortages are manufactured to control people, so they are seldom real.

PROJECT THE CORRECT PICTURE

Are you projecting the picture of what you want to have *manifest (show up)* in your life? Are you the master of your destiny or are you a so-called "victim of circumstance?" and just along for the ride.

You are a creator and are orchestrating everything that happens to you through your beliefs, ideas about your life, and expectations.

We are not just isolated bits of protoplasm, all alone and unimportant. We are human beings with a large aura of energy that circulates and interacts with everything and everyone else. Every thought, action, and desire affects the whole Universe at all levels.

Why am I telling you this? Because you are a creator and are orchestrating everything that happens to you through your beliefs, ideas about life, and expectations.

There is no such thing as being a victim, having an accident, or bad luck. Everything that happens to you is there for a reason. It is a learning experience, not bad luck or good luck, you did exactly what was necessary to make it happen, whether you knew it or not.

YOUR THOUGHTS AND EXPECTATIONS (BOTH POSITIVE AND NEGATIVE) SHAPE HOW THE WORLD RESPONDS TO YOU

You are not isolated. You affect what happens to you.

At some level of your psyche, even the subatomic level, you may have a little feeling of *not being good enough, not working hard enough, or not deserving more money.* You may have aligned with a *vow of poverty* from a past life. If you don't believe in past lives, that's okay. That belief in not enough may have come from a movie you saw or from the genetic link via DNA from your great-great-grand parent's belief.

Even if your idea of wealth is just enough to keep the bills paid you should not have to struggle for it.

These perverted beliefs are just like computer programs, working behind the scenes, directing the action in everyday life. If they are not erased and replaced with positive and beneficial programs, they sabotage all your plans.

These hidden programs dictate to the Universe the outcome in all aspects of your life. Change your thoughts-change your life!

Lack of adequate wealth is a sickness similar to all other diseases.

In our Cosmic Energetic Healing work, we look for and remove these little disturbances in the mind programs. We call them *energy blockages*. We replace them with a positive flow of energy in a healing matrix, plus we add beneficial affirmations in the present tense.

Lack of adequate wealth is a sickness similar to all other dis-eases. Health and well-being, not sickness and poverty, are natural to human beings. Those energy blockages push away good opportunities to make money. You could think of these programs as "junk software" in your computer.

Thoughts are things.

It is very difficult to get rich when you feel poor! What you send out comes back to you!

One of our clients, Bob, was about 50 years old when we met him. He was doing part-time mechanical jobs in his shop. Some people would not pay him, and others left their repaired equipment for months before they picked it up or paid. He was barely making a living.

Change your self-talk and your life will change.

One day I heard him tell a customer, *"I'm just a poor boy, and I don't have a lot of money."* Guess what? He was telling his subconscious mind how he expected his life to be. Your self-talk creates your future. I explained to Bob how he was programming his mind by telling it *he was only a poor boy.* Since *thoughts are things,* he could expect to continue barely scratching out a marginal living. He listened and changed his self-talk. Seven years later, he now calls himself a *master mechanic,* has multiple income-producing businesses, and is making five times more money.

People can follow the traditional right steps for success but fail because they believe that they will fail.

INCOME INCREASED BY 300%

Julie owns a sports-item manufacturing company and wanted a little more income. We helped her increase her sales 300% by giving her our two new words to say. When she changed her self-talk to include these two new words, she made three times more sales that year.

If you want your sales to increase, you might say: "I want to increase my sales!" That's a good starting point, but it will not increase your sales. Why not? Because you are coming from a place of lack. The underlying thought is *I don't have enough sales, and I want sales!* The universe hears *I don't have enough sales* and makes that statement true. The universe echoes back to you exactly what you send out. The feeling of not having enough money gets you more of . . . "not having enough money."

WORDS THAT PUMP THE MONEY!

If you retain only one idea from studying this manual, I hope it is the use of the magic words – EVEN MORE!

Can you lie to your subconscious mind and get results? No! Then what's the secret? The two little words that increased Julie's income 300% were *"EVEN MORE."* When you use these words, you aren't coming from a place of lack. You have some and are open to receiving even more. If you want money, you show the Universe that you already have some. Julie looked in her purse and took out some money. She looked at the money-nickels, dimes, dollars. It doesn't matter how much, as long as you have some. She learned to say, "I continually attract even more money and good customers."

GRATITUDE

When the money begins to flow in, it is very important to acknowledge the success of having even more money by celebrating, even if it is just a little trickle of more money at the start. Your celebration and show of joy is the fuel for attracting *even more money*. Emotion excites the subconscious mind into action. You can also use emotion when you say "thank you" after you start getting what you want.

EMOTION (E-MOTION) = ENERGY IN MOTION!

You have to prime the pump of abundance to get it flowing into your life. "Thank you for having brought me <u>even more</u> spendable cash money!"

The feeling of not having enough sales sends a message of lack out to the Universe.

Rev up your emotions. They are extremely important tools for manifesting. When you are stressed and depressed, you want even more out of life but are not allowing it to come in. The alignment exercise at the end of this chapter helps you open your heart to   receiving.

Is your conscious mind fighting your affirmations?

SAMPLE AFFIRMATIONS FOR PROSPERITY

• I am always in the right place at the right time for *even more* good opportunities.
• I attract even more opportunities for my successful businesses.

- I am open to receiving even more abundance in all areas of my life.
- I am open to receiving even more spendable cash money.
- I am at one with a tremendous amount of money.
- I deserve even more wealth and affluence.
- All the things I am seeking, and even more, are now FINDING me!
- I am <u>in the process</u> of becoming even more wealthy.

Even your conscious mind can agree when you say you are "in the process" of becoming even more wealthy, etc.

Controlling your consciousness is an ongoing process. Even as teachers, we constantly focus our attention on "bringing even more success and joy into our lives." And it works!

Remember that health and well-being (wealth and abundance) are natural to you. You have to push them away to experience lack and so-called bad luck. You do this by holding on to hidden negative emotions and using negative self-talk.

To get a real understanding of how to use your constant natural self-talk for your benefit get Shad Helmstetter's book, "What to Say When You Talk to Yourself."

Energy clearings help get rid of feelings of unworthiness, disapproval of self, and being undeserving of abundance. Positive affirmations in an energy matrix redirect the energy to accomplish your goals and to bring even more abundance into your life.

ALIGN YOUR POLARITY

An exercise to align your energy with the universe and the earth, and to open your heart to giving and to receiving.

A PRACTICE FOR ALIGNING AND INCREASING YOUR ENERGY

Here's a method of aligning your body, mind, and spirit's polarity that we developed in our Cosmic Energetic Healing seminars. We found that energy healings work much better when the individual is grounded and aligned with the healing centers of both the Earth and the   cosmos.

THE BULL STORY

Aligning polarity reaffirms the hookup you naturally have with the Source of all life (your energetic home) and with the Earth from which your body is made.

Animals need this alignment, too! We learned this method while we were healing a sick bull with Reiki energy treatments. The original bull had done his job in the spring and the owner had taken him away. Early that winter he purchased a young, eager bull. The old cows were already bred and not interested in the young bull. I think they wouldn't put up with any of his bull. The owner found him down (on the ground) one day and called us over to help. He acted like he couldn't get up. We suspected he'd been kicked by one of the cows.

We performed a remote Reiki healing on him (from about 25 feet away) and he got up, but he didn't stay up. We performed several more healings on him but found that they only held for a few hours. Something was wrong. I used muscle testing and found out that the bull was not grounded to the Earth and was not connected to the source energy for bulls.

We developed a technique to "align polarity" and used it on the bull. He got up after we aligned his polarity, and we didn't have to go back anymore. He was fine. We use this technique with great results with clients, and we teach it to our students. Healings stick 40% better when it is used. Try it for yourself.

POLARITY ALIGNMENT -- LONG VERSION:

1.   Take a deep breath. With your hands, pull a sample of energy out of your chest or heart area. Roll your hands around, as if you are rolling a ball in your hands. You are rolling the energy into a ball.

By aligning your energy, it makes life's problems seem very small.

2.   Send the ball of energy down, in a clockwise manner, to the center of the Earth. Make a hand motion round and round in the direction of a clock. Say, "I am aligning this energy with all that is healing and nurturing in Mother Earth. I am grounding my energy with the Earth grids. Mother

Earth is transmuting and healing all negative energy."

You are connecting yourself with the Source of all life and Earth — the 2 fields of energy that support and sustain you.

3. Bring it back into your hands. Send it in an upward motion to the center of the Source of all life in a clockwise motion. While it is at this highest frequency, put affirmations into it. Say, "I am putting love, joy, freedom, harmony, peace, abundance, prosperity, affluence, rejuvenation, and regeneration into my energy at the cellular level."

4. Bring it back down and explode it throughout your body! With your hands, pat this new and enhanced energy all over your body's energy field.

5. Take several deep breaths, aligning the new energy with your body, mind, and spirit.

THE SHORT VERSION -- Do this several times a day.

1.   Stand with your hands together in front of you in a prayer position. Slide your left hand up and your right hand down. They are pointing up and down now. Return to the prayer position.

2.   Reverse the slide movement. The left hand goes down and the right hand goes up. Return to the prayer position.

3.   From the prayer position, start pulling the hands apart. The left hand moves to the left, and the right hand moves to the right until they are outstretched to each side of your body at chest level.

4.   Great! Take a deep breath, allowing your energy work to settle into your body's aura and energy field.

You are one with the Source of All, and your body is from the Earth. The alignment reconfirms this connection.

Repeat this sequence, this time make a "ssssh-ing" noise (an energy movement sound) each time you move the hands up, down, or open.

You have successfully aligned your energy with the Earth and the cosmos. Plus, you have opened your heart for both giving and receiving.

Every time you do this, you increase your energy, healing your energy and aligning it with any words you say, such as even more abundance, even more prosperity, even more affluence, even more love, even more joy, even more health, even more fun, etc.

DRAWINGS OF ALIGNMENT EXERCISE
by Yolanda Eldora - artist and advanced student of Laser
Reiki and Cosmic Energetic Healing

4

WHY YOU HAVE WHAT YOU HAVE

AND KEEP GETTING WHAT YOU'RE GETTING

MOST PEOPLE'S EDUCATION TEACHES THEM LIMITATIONS

Because of the way most of us are raised and trained by our parents and teachers, it is almost guaranteed that we will cancel out our success before it gets to us. Instead of teaching us how to attain success, they constantly bombard us with all the reasons why we can't have it. We are told that a good education is necessary, followed by a good job. We are never encouraged to use our imagination. Do you remember being told, "It is just your imagination?" It's as if the imagination is not important.

Imagination is your ability to create an image of anything in your mind, even if it has never existed before. Without our imagination, we would never have even created the stone axe.

Many people work hard to heal their poverty.

If we make it to kindergarten with an active imagination, the keepers there do their best to ax it before grade school. We are taught to conform rather than create.

The problem is that their poverty is alive and well — it doesn't need healing. Heal the mind, and the poverty has a natural death as prosperity takes over.

Our ability to imagine, and therefore our talent for thinking outside the box, are all-important if we ever expect to go from poverty to plenty. Very few self-made millionaires have much formal education. That gives you a clue about our educational system and its aims.

We have been miseducated in many ways to keep us in the box. There are hundreds of books and studies about the evils of government education, we're not going to debate that in this manual.

Neither government schools nor fancy universities prepare you for creating prosperity or success.

It is your job to find out what successful men and women have done, and to follow in their footsteps.

Your education is an ongoing process. Just because you graduated from high school or college does not mean that you have any of the education necessary to attract prosperity. Traditional education does not prepare you for success. It prepares you to be a good little 9-5 slave.

You must prepare yourself for success by using your imagination, asking questions, finding answers, and never giving up.

Our abilities to imagine, and therefore our talent for thinking outside the box, are all-important if we ever expect to go from poverty to plenty.

According to Roi, there are only five things a student needs to learn from formal schooling:

1.   How to read, write, and spell words correctly.

2.   How to speak and express ideas fluently.

3.   How to do math and count your money.

4.   How to look up information.

5.   How to talk to your subconscious mind. (Anyone can do this with training. See Chapter 8.)

Roi explains his views on education: "Anyone can become truly self-educated with the above skills, which could be learned in a maximum of three years, (rather than the traditional 12 to 22 years), if you left out the propaganda, indoctrination and baby-sitting while both parents work. Without teachers telling you that things are impossible to accomplish, you can easily think outside the box. If you are able to think outside the box, you might find real, useable wealth. Designing nonpolluting energy systems could be a snap.   The secrets of nonpolluting and renewable power supplies would be with the many rather than the   few."

If you have ever seen lightning, you know electricity is all around us and it is absolutely free.

Of course, it can be harvested at the point of use. Those big batteries and charging stations are totally unnecessary and only need to be used to make money and have complete control of you.

HOW DREAMS ARE CANCELED OUT IN SEVEN SECONDS

In order to impress a desire upon the subconscious mind, you must hold that thought without canceling it out for 17 seconds.

We do several things that keep wealth and affluence away. The first one is self-talk. It axes our wealth. Imagine yourself seeing a really pretty new car. You say to yourself, "Man, I'd like to have one of those! But I can't afford it!" Your desire and admiration for a thing actually starts it moving toward you. Then your "But I can't afford it" pushes it away and cancels out you're having it. Do you see how that works? How many hundreds of times have you repeated that process and canceled out your dreams?

EXAMPLE

A new employee in a large company thought, "I 'd really like to have a new, dark-blue BMW, but if I got one what would (my family) (my boss) (my minister) or (my IRS agent) think?" See how each of those thoughts put a halt to your desire?

Social consciousness, fear of being out of the norm, the need to conform, fear of what others will say, all interfere with you attracting your desires. There are unwritten rules about staying in the pecking order. This is like keeping to your rank in the military. These dogmas are useless in the real world. (See Chapter 9 on dogmas and how to release them.)

THE PT CRUISER

Here are Roi's thoughts on manifesting: "I'd like to have a PT Cruiser at a sensible price, so I can easily pay cash for it. I know it's on its way to me because I've done nothing to block it. That PT Cruiser will arrive when the conditions are right." What I've done is expressed the essence of what I want the Universe to furnish for me. I haven't specified the price or how it's going to happen. I'll let all the details be a surprise. There is only one thing I'm certain of. That the Source of All will take care of my PT desire in a manner even beyond my wildest expectations. How do I know it'll happen? Because my desires are always satisfied, since I quit pushing them away harder than I pulled them to me.

MANIFESTING A COPY MACHINE

Roi and I have always been interested in information. Secret information, hidden information, practical information. We buy tons of books, reports, and newsletters. We copy information for our friends and students who might be interested. I think information is wonderful. Everything is out there, but not readily available to the general public. You can find it if you know where to look. (Asking for divine guidance in helping you find it is a good thing.) My inner spirit was never satisfied with government schooling.

Roi and I decided that having a copy machine in our home office was necessary. At one time, I even had an AB Dick printing press in our living room. We bought a large, used, document copier, and it was good for several years before it started breaking down. We hauled it out to Washington when we moved from Arkansas.

Five years later, it was breaking down every month. I spent hours replacing parts, just to have it stop printing again and again. Sometimes I didn't know what to do and had to take the machine two hours away to Portland, Oregon, to have it fixed. I did this for another year, back and forth to Portland.

You can manifest negative things.

This power system works without judgment.

Finally, the copy machine was just too much trouble and wouldn't stay fixed. We decided to buy another used commercial machine. I researched other brands and came up with a new brand I thought I wanted. I searched the classified ads until I found a used copy machine, I thought would fit our bill. I called and found it was sold. I searched until I found another ad. I called-the machine was still there. The man assured me that it was in great condition, and he wanted only $300 for it. It was inexpensive because he was moving to Alaska in a few days. I was preparing for a weekend show and only had half a day free. He said he would drive south down from Seattle, and I would drive north to Olympia to pick it up. We met in a parking lot. There was no place to plug the machine in. It was the brand

I wanted. I handed over the $300 in cash and took the machine home. I was feeling pretty good, because I thought it was a good deal.

We can't help manifesting.

It's our nature.

ANOTHER BROKEN COPIER!

Six days later, after the show, I had time to set up my new copier and try it out. I was amazed. It did not work! We found a local repair person in the yellow pages who would look at it if we took it into his shop. We watched him check it over as he shook his head. The bad news! It was junk, maybe worth ZERO to $15.00.

It's more fun when we're in control and get what we really want.

We had manifested another junk copy machine.

Hummm? How could this happen? We scratched our heads. I thought about the steps that led up to finding a copier. Where was I focusing my attention? Manifestation is a mechanical process. It is not a hit- and-miss ordeal. Was I focusing my attention on the old junk copier while I was looking for a replacement? You bet I was. And what did I find? Another junk copier! What could we do now? Moan and groan, or celebrate a perfect manifestation? You might ask, "How can you call getting another junk copier a perfect manifestation?" We got exactly what we were putting our attention on. – a perfect manifestation!

Be careful how you ask for what you want – you may get what you don't want!

We all bring experiences and material stuff into our lives. It is important to recognize the part that our thoughts play in bringing forth things we like and things we don't like. Instead of focusing on the old broken- down copy machine while I looked for a replacement, I should have taken the time to dream in the kind of copier I really wanted. How would I have done it differently? I would have written up all the attributes I wanted in the newer copier-great performance. I would have seen myself being very happy with the new copies. I would have imagined it printing beautiful page after beautiful page.

You have the power to choose your response.

You have the power to choose where to put your attention.

LAUGH, CRY OR CELEBRATE?

Now I had to decide, would I choose to receive the manifestation of the junk copier with joy? I could choose to blame myself, complain about "how I always have bad luck." I could have felt that I had been victimized by the man who sold it to me. He was in Alaska, and I had no phone number or address for him. I was stuck with the broken copier.

I decided to look for the benefits of my gift from the Universe. I say gift because everything that happens to me or to you is a blessing in disguise. You can choose to look beyond the obvious negative automatic response. This reverse manifestation has been a benefit to me, because I am now very careful where I put my attention. It was a great lesson, and it cost me only $300. It could have cost thousands. Both Roi and I decided that a celebration was in order, just as if we'd won the lottery.

ANOTHER LESSON IN FOCUSED ATTENTION

Keep your focus straight ahead toward your goal.

When I was learning to dirt-bike ride on a motorcycle, this lesson came up often. One day I was riding in the high mountain trails in Idaho on an old, washed-out logging road. Roi was riding ahead of me about 30 yards. We were heading downhill, and three-fourths of the road was eroded into a fairly deep, rutty ditch. The trail was wide enough for the bike wheels to safely pass, but I let my eyes wander into the ditch. That ditch looked scary and deep. As I looked at the hole, I felt my heart take a little leap, feeling the fear of what would happen if I fell into the abyss. Next thing I knew, I was in the ditch, completely out of control. Eating dirt is not fun! Roi finally missed me, turned around, and rode back looking for me. He asked, "Taylore, what are you doing down there? Why are you in the ditch?" I said, "I don't know." I was sore, bruised, bleeding, and scraped. And I needed help getting the bike back on the trail. I could barely ride back home.

Put your attention on where you want to go, not where you don't want to go.

Why did this happen? What was my lesson? Was this an accident? Coincidence? Bad luck? Was God punishing me? Am I a victim of circumstance? No! No! I just had another learning experience.

DON'T LOOK AT (put your attention) **WHERE YOU DON'T WANT TO GO.** (That sounds simpler than it is.)

I finally learned that I could only look at where I wanted to go. I had to keep my attention on the trail. I could not look at the ditch and other scary obstacles without going there. I've used those same lessons in other areas of life. There are obstacles everywhere. I've learned that they aren't important. Don't look at them. Don't tell your dreams to others.

Don't let other people or other things distract you from your dreams.

Keep your attention focused on your goal. Soon it will be yours

The truism here is to always put your attention on the things you want to achieve. Never focus on what you don't want because you will receive whatever you focus upon. What is the end result that you desire? Decide what it is that you desire and focus on the completion of that aspect only. Don't even speculate on how it may come about.

There are lessons everywhere.

IF YOUR ENERGY IS NOT RIGHT . . .?

Pay attention to what is happening around you.

A psychic who had worked for the US government came to the local metaphysical bookstore to put on a talk some years ago. The owners of the bookstore were friends of ours, and they invited us to come hear what he had to say. He had the ability to look at an individual's aura and read the status of their emotional and physical health. We went to him for an assessment of our health. He gave us a long list of expensive homeopathic drops we "needed" to take. We took his supplements without noticing much improvement.

You can do all the right things to ensure success, but if deep down inside you have feelings of failure, the project will ultimately fail.

Over the next few months, we became friends with him. By that time, the bookstore owners no longer liked him and wouldn't promote him. He asked me to do the advertising so he could put on a seminar. I'm good at setting up and advertising seminars. When his event came, he became very disappointed with us because only a few people showed up. He was mad at me. According to him, it was all our fault that so few people showed up. That was the end of the relationship.

What's the lesson here? When a person's energy is not aligned with success, it won't happen. Had he sabotaged himself through his thoughts, feelings, and expectations? Or did he really have nothing to offer attendees? On the psychic level, the audience had other things to do that evening. On the inner level, they were responding to the world by not showing up where they didn't need to be.

If people do not show up for your talks or seminars, there are three possible reasons:

1. Advertising problem: You have not let enough people know about the event. When all else is in alignment, it is a numbers game. If 20,000 are exposed to your ads, perhaps 10-20 will show up.

2. If the speaker isn't aligned with the audience, they can feel it at the subconscious level. The speaker may have feelings of not being good enough himself/herself. If that is the case, the Universe will not align them with great success.

3. The audience may not be attracted to the program.

IS YOUR LIFE ON REPEAT?

Have you noticed the same patterns repeating over and over in your life? Are you tired and bored by the same old stuff coming up? If so, you'll like this story about a mother and her house fires.

Ask and you shall receive.

One summer evening in 1986, Roi and I were sitting in the bleachers at the 1-30 Speedway near Alexander, Arkansas. It's one of the best auto-racing dirt tracks in the Southeast. During an intermission, the announcer said, "Blah, Blah, Blah . . . Mary Ballad and her children suffered a fire and lost all their furniture. If you have any extra household furniture you want to donate, come to the office. Leave your name and phone number."

I had found a home for the old furniture that renters leave when they move out. I hate to throw away usable things. I wanted the grounds of the mobile home park to look good. A pile of unwanted household goods is not very attractive. A few days before, I had wondered, "How am I going to get rid of this furniture?"

FIRE, FIRE, FIRE

Everything is drawn to you to learn from.

A few days later, Mary, arrived with a big truck. We had the furniture stacked on pallets under a large tarp. While Roi and I uncovered the treasure, I asked, "How did you come to lose all your belongings in the fire?" She said that this was the third fire she had experienced in the last three years, and that every time she lost all her stuff. She had no insurance.

It is good to pay attention, or you'll just get the same lesson over and over.

I am not good at holding my tongue when I get an urge to speak. I blurted out, "Isn't it time you quit having fires? Haven't you learned what you need to learn from this experience? Let it go! You can have a good life! You don't have to keep having the same experience over and over again!" She was so shocked to be talked to like that, she had nothing to say. She must have been spellbound at the idea that she could control her life. She had a surprised look on her face but said nothing.

When you get "in the zone" as athletes say, you know that you are going way beyond where the conscious mind could take you.

You are accessing your unlimited self.

She looked at me strangely several times, as she took the whole pile of furniture except one broken item, which we tossed in the Dumpster. She seemed to want to ask me more, would start to speak, then shrug. I know she will never forget the experience, and neither will I.

Spirit "came over me" and put those words into my mouth. It was like I was channeling a message for Mary. I'm usually not very forward around strangers. I felt the air thick with higher source energy. I was used by this higher presence to deliver a message to the three-times fire lady. I noticed that my energy was especially high, and I was spaced out all that afternoon.

I checked on her, ten years later. No more fires. Were her fires an accident? Or were her fears drawing into her life the same fire experience over and over?

Sometimes we need a little extra help to get rid of repeating negative patterns.

WE WERE LED!

A number of life experiences led us to develop our Cosmic Energetic Healing techniques. Using these methods, you can easily identify, release, and heal negative habits and patterns. You then install new, positive affirmations within an empowering energy matrix. When these techniques are used, the new habit installed becomes effective immediately. Anyone can energetically heal relationships, illness, pain (even chronic pain), emotional problems, lack of money, bad habits, and karma with a weekend of training. Additional information about the energy healing school and the Reiki Ranch, in Chehalis, WA, and its classes are located at the end of the manual and on the Web site: *https://LaserReiki.com*

List three lessons you have learned from negative situations:

_____

_____

_____

_____

_____

_____

Would you have learned these lessons otherwise?
Explain:

_____

_____

_____

_____

_____

_____

Think BIG! As master Yoda said, "Size matters not!"

5

WHAT IS MONEY?

AND HOW TO GET WHAT YOU WANT

IS MONEY GOOD OR BAD?

What is a Federal Reserve note? Could you really be paying all your debts with IOUs?

Do you want money? What is this thing called money that we all desire and need? It is a piece of paper that you trade for things. According to the writing on its face, it is a note. A note means that you owe money. Boy, that's confusing. It is stored energy. Money is not bad, but some people think it is. If you think that money is bad, then your thoughts will push it away.

For instance, most patriots are broke because they hate the evils of federal reserve notes. They long for real money, as required by the Constitution-gold and silver. The next-best solution would be paper money that represents the actual amount of gold and silver stored in the country's vaults. Money would then have value behind it.

If banks create money out of thin air, then why can't you attract it with your thoughts?

Today's money is not backed by gold or silver. They can print as much as they like. Banks make money out of thin air and computer bits. Bankers just make data entries and create loans you have to pay back with substance and the sweat of your brow. They don't even have to depend on printed money for their supply.

THINGS YOU MAY NOT KNOW ABOUT $$$

I'll show you how our American banking system works. A young family has saved a down payment and goes to the bank to apply for a home loan. The bank decides that they earn enough money and have good credit, so they loan the family $110,000 to buy their first new home. The banker does not run downstairs and look into the vault to see if the bank has $110,000 to loan out. The money to loan is invented by a few strokes of the keyboard on their computer screen the moment the couple's application is approved.

Licenses give you permission to do things that would otherwise be illegal to do. Obviously, banks need a license.

Next, the bank is listed as first lien holder on the couple's home. The new home is now property owned by the bank. The bank has an asset it didn't have before-the couple's new home plus their $15,000 down payment. If the couple does not make the payments, the bank repossesses the property. The bank's total cost was only slightly more than the cost of doing the paperwork. The bank wins because they never did loan the couple any money. They only loaned them computer bits.

BANKS CREATE MONEY!

The bank financed the home by the loan officer typing numbers into the computer. Now the bank has new collateral on its books -- the $110,000 home plus $15000 cash. With current rules, the bank can "loan" or create out of thin air, 8-10 times the $125,000 value of the home. Loaning money is a good business especially if you can create money like banks and credit card companies do.

Do you limit the amount of air you breathe, so others can have their share of air, too?

Then why limit your income?

The above scenario is one of the reasons why NESARA (National Economic Security and Reformation Act) was passed. It has not been implemented yet. It will forgive all credit card and mortgage debts, recreate money backed by precious metals, restore Constitutional Law, abolish the IRS, and produce many more benefits, including more peace in the world. There is opposition to its implementation from the establishment. For more information on NESARA and the white knights, go to: *http://www.fourwinds10.com*

IS WORLD PEACE POSSIBLE?

Lama Tsering: "So, if just one person in a family practices kindness, soon the whole family will be more peaceful. Peace can grow from this-family to family, village to village, city to city, country to country. Kindness creates peace. Anger and hatred create suffering. We make the problems. We make the unhappiness. We can make kindness and happiness, too. Kindness is a responsibility."

Like more wealth in your life?

Study this manual every month until your mind is more open to receive.

ARE YOU OPEN TO RECEIVING MONEY?

Money represents stored energy from the source of all. It is made out of the same God stuff as all material things in the 3rd dimension. It doesn't matter whether it is created by bank's computers, is printed on paper by the US government, or is paper backed by silver and gold. The amount of money each of us can attract is limited only by how much stored energy we can accept. What keeps you from accepting more than you now have?

Do you think that you will be taking away from someone else if you decide to accept more? You won't! There is plenty to go around. Like I said, "Banks are creating it by the billions each day via their computers. The Treasury Department is printing it 24 hours a day."

Let go of the past!

Live in the now.

You can have as much money as you desire. So can your neighbors. There is no lack of money. The world is an abundant place. We limit ourselves through our thoughts about money.

ARE YOU IN HARMONY WITH YOUR DESIRE

When you know that you know, the universe often answers instantly.

Let's say you desire abundance. You must be in agreement with your dreams and desires. What if you desire to have your own business, but you are not in harmony with that desire? What if you have deep feelings of not being "good enough" or the belief that you have to "work hard" before you can achieve the abundance you desire? Are your emotional feelings in conflict with your desire? That is usually the problem when you are not receiving what you desire. A good way to check this is to write down a dream or a goal on a yellow pad or in your workbook. Next, write a list of any feelings you feel in your body as you think about your desire or goal. The goal may seem a little scary at first. See if you can work through the fears and other unknowns with positive self-talk.

You deprive no one when you choose to accept even more abundance into your life!

The more you look at your dream, the more possible it becomes in your mind. The reason we could manifest the first double-wide mobile home is because we were familiar with them. Last year we manifested another double-wide, even better than the first, and it was given to us the first day my ad came out. We moved it to the Reiki Ranch and set it up as a triple-wide by adding a   6-foot center section with a cathedral ceiling and roof. A dozen high windows were installed to let in more light. It's awesome and the price was right-free!

More Yoda: "No try. Either do or do not."

"SIZE MATTERS NOT" - YODA'S COMMENTS

It doesn't matter what size your goal is. The universe does not limit you. A penny is just as easy as $10,000. It is all out of consciousness and energy in action.

Here's an example of how I walk through the steps in finding out what might be blocking my personal goals. You can do the same procedure for one of your goals and fill out a similar worksheet. This exercise will help you find the energy blockages.

I am getting my dream into my energy field.

EXAMPLE

My dream is to have alternative health/holistic healing centers where all modalities, including allopathic medicine, can be practiced.

1. My stomach says, "This is a little scary, because I have never thought about an idea so large   before." (I would talk to myself about these fears and see if I could reduce the stress associated with having a big project. I would assure myself that I would have plenty of help.)

2. My mind asks, "Who is going to give me $50 million for these clinics?" (I know that when I align my energies in a certain way, the universe will yield to me any desire or dream that I have. And that the right people will come along to support this plan. Some very rich people desire to lead healthy lives, also.)

I'm bringing the light of my dream into every cell of my body.

On the other side of the dream is the excitement of completion. (This is a good part.)

1. Wow! This dream will help so many people. People can have a real choice in selecting the nature and kind of treatment their bodies, minds, and spirits need. They are no longer stuck with the common toxic chemical, radiation, and other witchcraft treatments for cancer but can receive the education to help them make a choice. They do not have to go strictly with the AMA, which tries to

poison their bodies into wellness with drugs. (That is similar to trying to bomb a country into peace.)

There's plenty of room in my dream to accommodate some of your dreams.

Working together we can accomplish even more.

2.   All modalities of healers and energy workers will be invited. The body will be cleared of toxins within the physical tissues, the mind, and the emotions. The body will be pampered with spa treatments, massage, and other luxuries.

3.   Seminars and workshops will be ongoing for the clients' education in learning how to take care of the body through nutrition, self-improvement, empowerment for the mind, and spiritual enlightenment, as well as through pure recreation, learning, and practical exercises.

4.   I enjoy building and organizing. I can delegate to wonderfully inspired people who will help bring the dream into reality.

5.   I can see myself in the celebration of the completion of the centers, with a bright and beautiful light shining forth. I visualize it, I feel it, I accept it, it is mine. (Now I can go stand on a hill and scream the following words to the world!)

"I am me! I am free! I am wonderfully free of all limitations to receive this beautiful gift for me and for all the people who are helping with the centers and to help heal our wounded brothers and sisters. from all over the world.

I end procrastination by getting familiar with my dream.

"Thank You, God, for helping me to fulfill my dream even more fully than I could have possibly imagined. Thank You for bringing together all the wonderful healers of all modalities, administrators of the healing centers, tools, methods, designers, builders, financial funding, accountants, politicians, attorneys, government officials, naturopathy doctors, medical doctors, medical diagnostic tools, equipment, and whatever else will be needed."

IT IS NOW YOUR TURN

Write your own desire, dream, or goal:

Choose abundance, prosperity, success, harmony, freedom, love, etc., or a combination.

My dream is:

_____

_____

_____

_____

_____

_____

1.   My stomach (gut mind) says:

_____

_____

_____

_____

_____

_____

2.   Other fears I am feeling:

_____

_____

_____

_____

_____

_____

3.   My conscious mind says:

_____

_____

_____

_____

_____

_____

4.   I'm worried about:

_____

_____

_____

_____

_____

On the other side of my dream is   excitement:

Success begins with reprogramming the mind in the direction that you choose.

1. Wow! This dream will:

_____

_____

_____

_____

_____

_____

2. And I'm excited because:

_____

_____

_____

_____

_____

_____

Choose joy, love, peace, fun, well-being.

3. And I feel great about:

_____
_____
_____
_____
_____
_____

4. I see myself enjoying:

_____
_____
_____
_____
_____

Express gratitude and blessings for the completion of your project as if it is finished.

5. I celebrate the successful completion of my dream because I already see results, such as:

_____

_____

_____

_____

_____

This is powerful.

Hooray! Yippee! Yahoo!

Express blessings and gratitude!

You are saying that you know it is a done deal. Celebration is a way of signaling the Universe that you are ready to receive and see it as completed.

As you practice writing down your dreams in this detailed form, you can work through the fearful and scary parts. That will help you discover the areas where you're not in harmony with your dreams. Once you realize where you are not in harmony, you'll find the energy blockages easier to clear. The joy and expectation of the completion will gain momentum as you see it as a done deal.

If one of us can do it, then we all can do it. That means you, too, can do it!

Others have done it and you can, too! You can do it. I'm counting on you to choose to take charge of your life and your thoughts, and therefore become the master of manifestation that I know you to be because all humans are creators.

THOUGHTS AND BELIEFS

If you want to change your financial position, you must first check out your thoughts and beliefs. Since you are reading this manual, chances are you desire to have a more-compelling future with lots of money and thoroughly enjoy being jobless. In order to alter your outer experience of life, first you must change your inner experience. The inner I am referring to is your thoughts. You can change your thoughts, and then change how you talk to yourself-your self-talk. When you change your thoughts, your outer world changes. It may take time and it will take effort.

You have the power to choose your thoughts.

You are a much-higher power than your thoughts, and you have the power to choose them. They will obey you when you are persistent. You are a spiritual being playing like a hopeless human. When you take charge of your thoughts, you are a spiritual being playing like an affluent, wealthy, human being. That's a role I bet you could learn to enjoy. We have!

REALITY IS MALLEABLE

Lighten up on yourself.

You create your reality through your thoughts and beliefs. Beliefs are just habits of thinking. If you keep thinking the same thought over and over, you create a belief. Whether it is "right" or "wrong" isn't relevant. What matters is what you are thinking. Become aware of what you are thinking. If your thoughts benefit you, great. If not, choose more uplifting thoughts.

Judging yourself will only pull you down in energy frequency.
Make changes rather than judgments!

WITHOUT MONEY, IDS, OR CREDIT CARDS

While attending one two-week Tony Robbins NLP seminar, we had to give the promoter all our ID cards, all credit cards, and all our money. They gave each of us back a quarter and an apple. We had to go to a city 85 miles away, do someone a service, and return in 18 hours. They sent us out about midnight, and we had to be back at the seminar by 6:00 p.m. the next day to report in. Most of the 600 participants did well. Very few had problems, most ate well and enjoyed the outing. One fellow came back from Houston in a limousine, another flew back from Fort Worth in a chartered airplane. The quarter was for a telephone call if all else failed.

Whether you have $$$ or not, know that you are fully supported by the universe.

Roi and I had our motorcycle helmets in our motor home and picked them up before we headed out to hitchhike toward the 1-35 freeway. It was wild with 600 people trying to hitchhike from the hotel in Austin. Our carrying the helmets implied that our bike had broken down and we needed a ride. It took us one ride to get to the freeway in Austin, where we headed south. It took us two rides to arrive in San Antonio. We walked to the River Walk and found a table and chairs along the walk. We decided to put on a quit smoking cure as our service. We visited a hotel, where we borrowed   poster making materials at someone's seminar, plus received a free lunch at the event going on. We were all set to offer our services to the tourists who walked by our table along the River Walk. We helped people until about 2 PM, then started walking back along the interstate from downtown San Antonio.

Money (coupons of source energy) are easier to carry than a cow.

A biker in his pickup truck saw us hitchhiking, picked us up, and drove us to the hotel in Austin. On the way, he took us to his home a couple blocks from where he picked us up and gave us some snacks. He figured out that we didn't have a bike, and there were far too many people hitchhiking on the freeway. We finally told him that we were part of a seminar testing our skills for survival in real life. He was more than happy to spend an afternoon chauffeuring us 87 miles back to Austin. He seemed to enjoy exchanging ideas and being with people who thought outside the box.

The secret is to not only survive but to flourish in all circumstances.

Even without money, certain individuals will flourish. It depends on your attitude. Choose an attitude that supports your new holistic belief system.

Release struggle, embrace flourishing. And enjoy the Journey.

MONEY, CASH, DOLLARS, COINS, CHECKS, MONEY ORDERS, COMPUTER BITS, etc.

We quit surviving several years ago. Now we flourish! (An example of self-talk.)

We find that many people are afraid to carry large amounts of cash. Some carry just a few dollars and cents, plus their charge cards. If you have even a little bit of fear about carrying money or owning cash, you probably have a fear of receiving money or a fear of losing dollars.

The media pounds us with stories about muggers, thieves, and scams taking away our hard-earned cash. There are elements in our government and banking concerns that would like to see us as a cashless society. They would have full knowledge and complete control over all our transactions.

Fear of having cash sends a message to the subconscious mind that it isn't safe to have cash.

Therefore, you will seldom receive cash.

Personally, I don't like that idea, and I don't give it any energy. Instead, I embrace what freedom feels like, what expansion feels like. They feel good! That is where I go. I don't go where it feels dark and suppressed. I have the personal power to choose where I put my thoughts. That's where I go. That's why I consistently manifest on the positive side. I put my energy where it does the highest good for all concerned, including Mother Earth and her healing needs.

If you still can't squelch your fear of having cash, see your money arriving as checks, money orders, bank drafts, lottery tickets, sweepstakes, gifts, or bank transfers. If you do not release your unease about receiving cash, the money won't come. Give it another route or get used to carrying cash. We started carrying even more cash some years ago. I've always had some cash in my pockets. Now I have even more.

On this page keep track of every payment you make in cash, check, or credit card. Do it at the moment. Where is the money drain? If there is a problem, it will show up on this list. (Buy a small notebook and take it with you to keep track.)

Day Amount Spent How Spent (essential or nonessential)
(donation or fun)

___ _____ _____

___ _____ _____

___ _____ _____

___ _____ _____

___ _____ _____

___ _____ _____

___ _____ _____

___ _____ _____

___ _____ _____

___ _____ _____

___ _____ _____

___ _____ _____

_____ _____ _____

_____ _____ _____

_____ _____ _____

_____ _____ _____

_____ _____ _____

_____ _____ _____

_____ _____ _____

_____ _____ _____

_____ _____ _____

_____ _____ _____

_____ _____ _____

_____ _____ _____

_____ _____ _____

_____ _____ _____

_____ _____ _____

_____ _____ _____

NOTES:

6

HOW TO NOT CANCEL OUT YOUR SUCCESS

HOW TO GET WHAT YOU WANT

A BROKEN HIP WAS BAD NEWS. FROM BAD NEWS COMES GOOD

In 1981 I was on a speaking circuit with Roi when I received word that Wally, my mother, had broken her hip and was in the hospital. She was not liking it very much and didn't understand why her hip had broken. She was mad about being in the hospital and mad at me because I wasn't there with her. I said, "Wait a minute. Have you ever considered that everything negative that happens to us is a gift?" Wally replied, "Well, I never thought about it that way."

Consider everything that happens to you as a gift, including bad news.

I've always found this to be true in my life. I assumed this to be true for her. I told her, "Look around. Something very good is going to happen as a result of your visit to the hospital." Looking for a miracle gave her something to do. As the days passed, she became good friends with a nurse.

The nurse, Jewel, and her spouse were looking for a place to park their double- wide mobile home. Wally told her about their beautiful park with the big oak shade trees. The park was very private, located in the country, but close to town. Jewel and her spouse moved into the park. They were great friends with my parents for five years. When both my parents got sick, Jewel was right there helping them out with her nursing skills. Jewel was the perfect gift from the universe. Thank you, God, for sending this *Jewel* to Wally.

HOW TO CHANGE YOUR MOOD

You don't want to create your dreams while you are in an unhappy state.

Sometimes you may find yourself in a bad mood. Don't despair. It is only a temporary condition. What's the one thing you never want to do while in a bad mood? Manifest. Why is that? Like attracts like. The feelings that you send out are the feelings you attract back. It's the Law of Attraction. You don't want to create your dreams while you are immersed in an unhappy spell, The results would be counterproductive. Spend as little time as possible in unhappiness, gloom, and doom. I don't spend much time watching TV or news because it makes me feel unhappy. I'm not suggesting that you be bubbly and ecstatic all the time. Neutral, peaceful, content, joyful, or playful would be nice and a great help to you.

The feelings you send out are the feelings you receive back, because of the Law of Attraction.

HOW TO SHIFT FROM SADNESS TO HAPPINESS

Look at your posture. Is it slumped? Do you feel sad? Pull your posture back into a more erect position. Sit up straight in your chair. Pull your shoulders back while you move. Put a smile on your face. It may feel strange at first. Keep doing it. You won't break. Wiggle your face and open your eyes. Put another smile on. Breathe deeply, feeling the fresh air invigorate your body. Breathe out stress, anxiety, and worry. Breathe in peace, well-being, and harmony. Do this three times. You should feel much happier.

Realize that sadness is a temporary state that you cause by "your" thoughts. The real you (Soul) is a happy entity. You are just letting the outer world get to you.

USE YOUR MEMORY

Think of a time when you were happy. Remember what you were doing, how you were feeling. A real smile is starting to grow on your face. This is called *jump-starting* your emotions. You could also see a picture in your mind of something funny or of someone who brings you joy. As you remember that person's face, you can actually go back in time and feel the joy coming through that individual.

Childlike wonder is a great tool for manifesting.

I remember my granddaughter, Alex. When she was one to three years old, she sent me balls of pure source energy. They would come out of her eyes, face, and chest with such delicious pureness that the energy would almost knock me to my knees with joy. I still get goose bumps and a burst of joy thinking about that. How could I be in a bad mood when I just received such a joyful gift from the Creator Source, delivered to me through this small child? The faces of small children reflect the connection we once had with source energy, which continually flows from the source of all life.

Where did our natural joy go? How did we lose the dream? How do we find it again?

The Bible says, "Become like little children again." Children are optimistic and curious before kindergarten. They have high expectations of life. They are born knowing their importance. They know that they deserve abundance. It is their inheritance.

The universe yields to your desires, when your attitudes match these:

- Childlike wonder!

- Open to change!

- Lead by Spirit!

- Appear to be confident! (Act as if!)

- Act rather than react!

YOU CAN FLY FIRST CLASS

My friend, Rebecca told me about her trip to New York. She flew coach class from Seattle to New York City. She had a scary experience with noise and vibration around the window where she sat. This was so unpleasant for her, that she decided she would fly back home in first class. During the week that she vacationed in New York, she enjoyed dozens of peak experiences.

Anything is possible when your energy is aligned with your desire!

While standing on top of the Empire State Building, she felt expansive and wonderful. This was a time of feeling good, and the perfect opportunity to announce to the universe that she would be flying back home "first class."

Guess what? She asked, by making that declaration. The universe answered and the airline provided. The airlines offered Rebecca a chance to opt out of her regular flight back home-it just "happened" to be overbooked. In appreciation for the favor, she did them, the airlines upgraded her seat to a first-class passage at no extra charge. She arrived at her home airport at the same time as she had originally planned and was picked up by Tom, her spouse. She flew first class because the Universe yielded to her dream.

How did she manifest the first-class upgrade without having to purchase another ticket? Rebecca only thought about her desire when she was in a great mood!

What if you don't have the luxury to choose a peak mood in which to create your desire? What if you only have an hour to manifest an international ticket on an airplane?

MANIFESTING YOUR DESIRES UNDER PRESSURE

If you say, "This is bad!", it will not improve.

It is locked into being bad by your thought declaration.

Have you ever had the sickening feeling that you've missed your flight? Here's my story that illustrates the power of manifesting.

> *I'm in the Tocumen, Panama's international airport terminal. My bags have been checked curbside, and my daughter has driven away. I find out that my flight was **yesterday**! "You're **sure** it's not today?" I asked the attendant. Today's Houston flight is overbooked, and the lines are full. What a mess!*

> *What can I do? I can't go back to my daughter 's house, because this is the first weekend in her adult life free of kids and husband. My cousin, Holly, is waiting for me in Houston. And in two days, in San Antonio, I have a radio interview and demonstration on Instant Pain and Depression Relief.*

I am going to Houston! There are no other options. I have to be there. With my skills in consciousness and energy, manifesting, Laser Reiki, and Cosmic Energetic Healing, manifesting a desirable outcome from this mess should be easy. Now, in my mind I see Holly smiling and waving at me as she meets me at the airport, and I am two steps on my way to Houston!

If you don't take the situation personally (have judgment), then it is free to change.

I interrupt the story to show you that, here, we see the first steps to manifestation.

The steps I used to get to Houston

The Steps As illustrated in this story:

Decide upon a desired outcome.
1. I'm going to Houston, today!
2. Visualize it; see it as an accomplished fact.
3. I see Holly picking me up at the International Airport atHouston
4. Be grateful for the desired outcome.
5. Thank You, God, for helping me realize that You have already taken care of my arrival in Houston today, even beyond my wildest imagination!
6. Celebrate!

It has all worked out. It's a done deal!

Yaaaayyyy!

Now let's return to the story. . .

My manifestation list is ready, and I've done the first two steps.

I just need to keep from thinking of things that I **don't** want to have happen. Or dwelling on the circumstances that "made" me miss the flight. "How stupid I was to arrive at the airport a day late. " Thinking and saying things like that will cancel out the positive manifestation. For that reason, I choose to think happy thoughts.

All is in Divine Order!

No matter what it looks like at the moment. There is no point in worrying and fretting. Those useless thoughts will keep me upset and ruin my manifestation.

ONCE THE MANIFESTATION GOES OUT, DO NOT THINK ABOUT IT

I have come to realize how really important it is to be in gratitude for the things I don't like because I've yet to understand what the hidden gifts are.

And especially do not think about the worst that might happen. In this case, going back and ruining my daughter's free weekend, paying $1,200 for a one-way ticket to Houston, and missing my radio interview in San Antonio. If you think about the negative aspects, you cancel out all the good work you've done in manifesting.

To keep my mind off negative thoughts, I reach into my pocket for the photo of my youngest granddaughter. She is quite a beauty, and a capable Reiki Master at age six. Alex is an Indigo Child. Looking at that picture gives me great pleasure. I found it in my daughter's car while we were on the way to the airport. She had recently replaced photos in her wallet with new ones, and this picture was right there waiting for me on the seat.

In my purse I have a small book, *Silent Power*, by Stuart Wilde. Reading is a good way to keep the mind busy. Now, I've been in the airport for an hour; it's time to reaffirm my manifestation. This time I asked my angels for help.

I reaffirm my request and add:

• I will get to Houston without having to pay any extra money.
• And-I will fly first class!

Well, why not? Why settle for only getting to Houston? Let's travel in grand style. Life is an illusion. I asked myself, "Why not have a first-class illusion? Rebecca asked and got hers." I can fly first class, too!

I'm figuring that this is all a setup by my spiritual guides to test me. Will I walk my talk? Or will I crumble under pressure?

If you have bad luck, just look around.

There is some reason for you to be where you are.

Expect a miracle.

Reading the words in a book and manifesting in the third dimension are two different things. Add the pressure of a real-life emergency to the situation and the emotions boil unless you step back and look at the situation from outside the emotions. Manifesting is a mechanical process if you have all the steps.

It is not so important what happens but how you feel about it.

I teach manifestation, but I've never done it under pressure before. I pulled out fear and worry from my psyche and replaced them with peace using Laser Reiki techniques. I see myself flying first class, feeling the joy, imagining that I'm on the plane and relaxing knowing that all is in my angels' hands. I'm home free.

I did not feel like a victim because I missed the fight.

The airport line is thinning. Only the problem flyers, like me, are still here. I get shuffled from counter to counter. When I'm threatened with having to pay extra, I tell the agent, "I don't want to do that. See what you can work out." Finally, an agent asks if I would fly to Newark, New Jersey, and then hop a flight to Houston later in the evening. "Okay!" I cheerfully respond.

It was more of the "childlike wonder," but with a definite outcome in mind.

After five minutes of paperwork, I was off to the gate. I'm the last passenger to board, and the flight attendant said I could sit in first class because there were two empty seats there. (One of my desires was completed!)

I was in the first-class aisle looking over the two seats to see which one I wanted. One seat was back in the corner and looked dark. The other was the first seat on my right and it looked bright. I usually don't like to sit in the first row on airplanes because there is no place to put carry-on bags. Oh well, after all I'd been through, I was going to choose a seat in the light. (Later, I congratulated myself for this choice.)

I like the book, The Trick to Money is Having Some by Stuart Wilde.

He says, " In order to become wealthy you are going to have to become good at accepting things- very good. By accepting yourself, that becomes easier."

The businessman sitting next to me was pleasant, and we began to talk about Panama. He asked if I knew his friend - she's from Oklahoma but used to live in Panama, he said. I didn't know anyone from Oklahoma, but I asked, "What's her name?" Annie Cisneros. She was my very first friend when I moved to Panama where I lived for twenty years! We lost contact after I moved to the States. While I was visiting my daughter and her family, I tried, futilely, to find an address or phone number for Annie. My seatmate had dated her daughter for years.

We exchange lots of stories about Annie and her children. Like me, Annie is from Arkansas. If I hadn't asked for the name, the conversation would have ended.

Be present in the moment and open at all times to what the Universe is presenting to you or you might miss an important lesson.

The trip to Newark was great; the hours passed in no time. Thank You, God, for the extra bonuses of flying first class at no extra charge and finding out about my friend Annie! I arrived in Houston late at night, my manifestation complete. Holly picked me up at the airport -- just as I visualized!

Life can be great when you constantly thank the Source for all its opportunities!

Sometimes opportunities look like troubles. Just keep thanking the Source of all life, anyway.

It always works for me!

And it will work for you.

7

HIDDEN SECRETS IN PLAIN SIGHT

THE OBVIOUS UNOBVIOUS

AGELESS AND SECRET INFORMATION

How can I give you this ageless, secret information so that you will act upon it? This type of personal belief system has been hidden and passed down to only a select few. This is probably the most important information that you will ever read. It can and will change your life. But when will you realize it? Now? This year? Next year? Or even ten years from now? Does it matter, as long as it works?

What do you want out of life? Do you want money? Fame? Happy family? Health? Peace and harmony? Personal happiness? It is all available. It is only a heartbeat away. Through studying this manual, you will begin to change how you look at situations and how you feel about all that happens to you.

Beneath all material desire is the inner wanting of peace of mind, self-confidence, happiness, love, etc.

Most of us want money so we'll never have to worry about experiencing lack. We want a beautiful home and a beautiful family that we can adorn with lavish gifts. No debts! An abundance of money! Or at least enough money to take them out to dinner any time we want to. The cars are all paid for and running well. No major debts at all! Plenty of pocket money, some investments that double once or twice a year. Enough time and money to travel anywhere, any time. Good friends who think like we do, or at least who *think*.

You are learning to control your creation. Remember to take time for re-creation. Family, fun and play are most important.

You say that you want money, home, material things, but when you strip it down to the essence, you really want more peace of mind, self-confidence, love, joy, happiness, harmony, friends, adventure, and freedom. It is almost always the inner experience that you are looking for. Along the way, as you reach for and find those experiences, you will find the material things, i.e., job, house, car, etc. as side effects.

I've learned that being kind is more important than being right.

ACT INSTEAD OF RE-ACT

When you keep the altered ego low it's easy to be kind and gracious to others.

I've found that some people don't think much on their own. Believe it or not, most people do not act on their own either but react to outside influences. They run on old, self-defeating habits, childhood or past-life programs even if they don't believe in past lives, they are reacting to what others say or do. They spend most of their time *trying to please* others in order to be accepted into society or into their particular group. Look at the word react. Re-Act! They act in response to what they think others would want from them.

Ego is another word for Mind, inner self, Spirit and even God.

Their ego (altered ego is the correct term) may be higher than it needs to be. The high altered ego will demand too much control in their life. If so, it can get a person into control issues and easily get their feelings hurt. We have an exercise we teach at the retreats where the participants can check where their altered ego is on a scale from 1 to 10, 10 being the highest. Most people's altered ego runs around a 6 to 8. We've even found it at 10. We show them how to take it down to a 2. When the altered ego is too high (7 to 10) the person has to defend every word and every thought he has. People are overly sensitive, angry, arrogant, know it all, etc. They are not that much fun to be around. (See ego [altered ego] in next chapter.)

Ego is not a "bad word." The altered ego is "altered God," and should be taken down lower.

YOU CAN'T STOP CREATING

Each of us is creating life 100 % of the time. We each have all the necessary skills and create our reality 24 hours of the day. It is an automatic process. The power and ability are built into our human body/mind/system to create.

HOW DOES THE VICTIM ATTRACT RAPE?

Fear is a powerful emotion, and powerful emotions manifest easier than weaker ones.

By our thoughts, feelings, and beliefs we are sending out a set of parameters for manifestation. Look at the woman who fears rape. She creates a vibrational frequency of fear that she radiates to the universe. Fear is a powerful emotion. It stirs the quantum soup of which everything is made. Powerful emotions affect energy, matter, and time-the building blocks of the third dimension, our physical universe. Out there walking around near this woman's area is an equally powerful, vengeful man. The emotions of this man are not okay. He is depressed, angry, and believes he has been hurt by a female. He perceives he's the victim and thinks "poor me," "it's not my fault," "they have it coming to them" type thoughts. This mad-to-the-bone, frustrated man is looking for revenge - a victim to rape or worse.

The vibrational frequency predetermines the outcome.

It is no accident that these two individuals find each other. It's their destiny to meet. How does the predator find the prey? The prey emits a frequency the predator is seeking.

This all happens on the subconscious level (and the quantum level-way beyond the physical manifestations we are used to). These two frequencies have to attract each other. They are a perfect match like the two poles of a magnet. The woman's fear attracts the object of her fear, like Mary, the fire lady, attracted three home fires.

In another case, our client Penny feared rape and she had been raped three times, even once by her husband's friend. In a dream she was shown that her fears were attracting the very action she feared. We helped her clear her fear so she could break the chain of events. Part of her problem was karmic where it was revealed that she had been the abuser herself in many lifetimes where she was a man. One lifetime she was a soldier in ancient times. He had a very harsh, solitary life. After killing the enemy, they raped the women of the village and made them their slaves until they moved on. In this lifetime she had signed up to pay back that karma and learn compassion. After releasing these recurring patterns of attraction, she was free of the fear and no longer attracted rapes.

SUBCONSCIOUS MIND

First you must realize we have been lied to!

The subconscious is live and on duty 24 hours per day. It is also connected to all other subconscious minds, so all information that has ever been discovered is connected to it.

The conscious, on the other hand, is reactive, just like any personal computer, it waits for input to perform, and the evidence seems to show that most people have forgotten their password, so it seldom gets the input.

The subconscious makes it true using the orders it is given by your self-talk as well as what you give it on purpose, so watch both your inner and outer talk.

The person who thinks things will always go wrong, 1s right-things will always go wrong. Martin the investor had done all the right investigations, hired all the right people to ensure that his investment would be safe, and then it went wrong. Well, somewhere in his thoughts, feelings, and belief system he had the nagging feeling that things will go wrong, and so they did. The Life Manager goes to great lengths not to disappoint you.

Thoughts, feelings, and beliefs affect the universe and will come back to us as a manifestation of that thought. The stronger the feeling of the thought, the more powerful the manifestation. The investor was a creator, as we all are. If he'd focused his creativity on peace, joy, and how he always wins, his results would have been different. Through muscle testing it was shown to him that he had negative mind programs stating, "You are a loser. You won't ever amount to anything." Both of these statements had been installed by a frustrated teacher in grade school and had never been deleted.

Many such programs are installed in our conscious at an early age by our parents, brothers, sisters, teachers, and of course, our friends.

Eastern religions teach, "The Law of Karma is cause and effect." Average people say, "What goes around, comes around." Fear goes out and is returned as the object of our fears.

How does it feel to have the higher consciousness taking care of you and all your needs?

Your self-talk is supported.

Your mind chatter will also manifest your fears.

When you feel broke that idea goes out and comes back as the experience of having even less money. The dark cloud of worry goes out and comes back as an attraction of even more problems to worry about. All this circle of reacting and causing more of the same old stuff over and over can be healed.

SELF-TALK IS IMPORTANT

In conversation we ask, "How are you?" You may reply, "I'm surviving!" or "I'm okay!" or "I'm great!" The Life Manager listens to your self-talk and makes it true. Be sure you listen to your automatic self-talk. Change it if it isn't doing you any good. Just listen to what others say about themselves, and you'11 see their internal programming. Much of our self-talk was learned when we were children. If we had really wealthy and successful parents, and spent time with them instead of nannies, then our self-talk is probably not bad and will attract more wealth.

How does it feel to be well taken care of financially?

(Don't just read the words - feel it!)

Notice how those people who talk about their problems all the time seem to attract even more problems. They seem to have an endless list of terrible (judgment) things happening to them. What you focus your attention upon will come to be. Why not control your thoughts to bring things you enjoy and watch the good times roll in? You are creators. You create your bad times as well as your good times.

To truly understand how important self-talk is get the book, "What to say When You Talk to Your Self" by Shad Helmstetter, Ph.D.

MENTAL FASTING

Note on mental fasting: If I'm not thinking negative thoughts then they will not be reflected back to me by the Law of Attraction.

Years ago, when I lived in Panama, besides working full-time and raising a family I was searching for meaning in life. I read every UFO and ghost book I could find. There weren't many English books in Panama, and soon I was searching again. I found the Silva Mind Control methods. I enrolled in all their seminars and could do the work just fine. Next, I found a spiritual path called Eckankar. I liked those people and their ideas a lot. They had a Friday fast like the Catholics. I had become a Catholic when I was 20 because I had married one from Panama. I thought both parents being the same religion would help the children. It would be hard enough for them since I was gringa (female for gringo-meaning American in Latin American lingo) and my husband then was a Panamanian. I was a star at the Friday fast or just eating fish instead of meat. The regular Eckankar food fast was too easy for me. I told my teacher so. Then she advised me about the mental fast I could do. I was excited since I am very mental and love a challenge. The mental fast meant to *think only positive and uplifting thoughts all day long.*

The obvious un-obvious.

One of the secrets is how the Law of Attraction works!

I developed a strategy for canceling out the negative thoughts. Sometimes I'd just say, "Cancel, cancel, cancel." Next, I would imagine the negative word written on a white board. I erased it with an eraser. I then thought of a positive way to express that same thought and rewrote it on the board. I looked forward to the Friday fasts. I liked the mental fast so much that I kept doing it day after day until I now hardly ever have a negative thought. If I have one, it doesn't last long.

EARTH IS ABUNDANCE

There is so much abundance here on Earth. There is no lack. There is no need to want. There is enough for you to have all you want. How can you find your way to it? Or better yet, how can you just release your resistance to receiving it? Practice the Law of Allowance. Allow the universe to gift you financial abundance, freedom, the perfect relationship, great sex, etc. Your thoughts, feelings, and beliefs will either bring what you desire or what you hate, fear, and worry about. (The subconscious mind sees no difference.)

Look at what you are projecting out to the world. Your beliefs will push away good if you don't feel worthy enough to receive it. Law of Attraction and how it works is one of the secrets hidden from the masses and downplayed in the popular press.

How in the world could a person experience lack when there is an abundance all around?

It has to be self-inflicted wounds.

Were you told or shown that you weren't good enough as a child? If that is the case, you will never feel good enough to receive. Part of your body/mind will push good away, just out of the reach of your fingertips. There is a way to correct this-read on.

DREAM YOURSELF INTO ABUNDANCE

Think of yourself surrounded by even more abundance. Everything you ever wanted, and more is all around you. All your dreams are hanging in the air around you, but they are just inches away from your fingertips. You are floating in it - The invisible life force, the Source of it all. What keeps you from opening up to receive it? This abundance is free and just there for the taking. Just because you can't see it doesn't mean you can't have it. Once you claim it, know it is yours, it becomes visible and "appears" and falls or manifests into this reality. Your creations do not deprive anyone else of theirs either.

Some of the reasons this abundance can't easily come into your life is because you have negative, self-limiting belief systems all around you. These beliefs and dogmas encase you, acting like a screen or filter. All the good you want and deserve by your birthright must somehow be filtered through this thick screen of limited   thought.

You may identify with some of these belief systems and feelings that hold you down. A partial list is printed below:

• Feeling of not being good enough, having negative self-judgment. (I believe these feelings are the original sin if there is one. Everybody seems to have these feelings at a very deep level. They need to be cleared.)

• Not having enough education. (Are you buying into popular propaganda? Read the biographies of those who've made it big. Many had very little formal education. They were simply able to think outside the box and educate themselves.)

What if all the good you were to receive had to be filtered through the following negative mind programs?

Pretty slim pickings!

• Don't talk to strangers. (This childhood protection is no longer needed in adulthood. Think of all those trying to be salespersons who still have this junk program running around in their heads. Do you still have this? If so, it can be uninstalled.)

• Feelings of not being worthy. (It may come from parents, teachers, peer groups, religions, etc. It gives a person low self-esteem.)

• Others have the breaks, not me. (The breaks are built in your consciousness. Thinking that you "never get breaks" will hold them away!

• Not loving self, not liking self, not approving of self. (Learn to love your self first. Now, uninstall the dogmas that keep you from approving of yourself.)

• Poor me and victim consciousness. (These are never true. These feelings come from the past and can be healed. They also go along with low self-esteem, and feelings of unworthiness.)

• Fear of change. (The only thing that is constant in the 3rd dimension is change! Learn to welcome change.)

• Beliefs in dogmas. (Are you accepting other 's unproven ideas as your reality? Dogmas keep you a slave. Uninstall every one of them you find! (More dogmas are found in the next chapter.)

• Not open to receive. (The heart area in your chest is closed, blocked to receive. Use the alignment exercise I taught you in chapter 3 to open the heart.)

• Not comfortable to receive. (Because of the above negative feelings, you aren't allowing yourself to receive even more of the abundance that awaits. You are a giver. There must be a balance between giving and receiving. Your job is to start opening-to-receive so you can be balanced between the two.)

The power to choose is part of my natural toolbox.

These recurring negative patterns are like an endless chain holding you down. These beliefs and feelings filter out much of the good you could receive. Negative thoughts are not only hanging around like a shield but will actually weigh you down. You begin to sink below the surface of well-being like a fishing cork in the water pulled down by lead weights. No wonder most humans have felt heavy, blocked, and frustrated. And this is just the tip of the iceberg.

I CHOOSE BECAUSE I CAN

As you come to terms with your own greatness, you will accept that you are good enough, worthy enough, you like yourself, you are open to change, and open to receive without negative judgment. Breathe! (Take a deep breath.)

Breathe in the goodness that resides in the center of your beingness. You will trust in Spirit (God, The Source, Universal Life Force Energy) to deliver you to the right place at the right time.

As your negative belief system changes to a positive one, the lead weights drop off the fishing cork and you rise to the surface of your well-being. You are instantly surrounded by little signs from your angels of their presence, signs of abundance, and the inner feeling that "all is good." You are again a creator of your own destiny. Choose the direction that brings you more joy.

"I choose" is a very powerful choice of words. Need I say more?

(The idea of *the cork that rises to the surface* is from *www.abraham-hicks.com* Thanks for Ester and Jerry's seminars, tapes, and books on abundance and constantly reminding us to just "let it in" and "to allow good to happen.")

When you release these recurring negative emotions/patterns, the invisible filter screen is being removed. Now the good stuff can come into your life. Keep reaffirming your new state of consciousness by repeating the affirmations below or make up your own.

Taking a deep breath of air, visualize it as golden bright light with the power to clear and release negativity. See the negativity (darkness) being pushed all the way out of your body. Replace any negativity in the body with this inner light by reaffirming the love, joy, peace, freedom, and kindness that resides in your inner being.

Read your list breathing in the golden bright light filling your body with this healing and creative energy.

When you use the words, "In the process," the conscious mind can't find any reason to negate your statement.

- I choose to release all negative thoughts and emotions.

- I choose peace and joy over anger.

- I choose to release all fear of success.

- I choose to release all fear of failure.

- I choose to accept even more of the inner guidance ever present in my life.

- More money is always coming my way. It's easy for me to attract even more money.

- I am in the process of becoming a millionaire.

- I am at one with all that is good.

- I am constantly expanding my personal understanding that there is more than enough for me.

- I am safe, whole, and complete.

- All that I am seeking is now finding me.

- I open my heart to receive even more love, good health, and abundance.

- I am divinely guided in every word, thought, and deed.

- I am a magnet of goodness, wealth, affluence, and abundance.

•I am creatively jobless, so I have free time to accept success.

•I AM, I AM, I AM, I AM

If you cannot imagine a perfect now with joy, well, I guess you can kiss the perfect future good-bye.

Fake it until you make it.
Act as if you already have it.
And — never give up!

We don't want the old habits of limiting belief to hang around, so it is a good idea to come back often to this list. Say your list at least twice a day for 21 days, then every day as you think you might need a tune-up.

LIVE   IN THE NOW TO INFLUENCE   THE FUTURE

Many mystics have said all is now. There is no past or future. All is in the present. Well, if you take care to choose even more joy in the present moment, the future will be assured to be in joy. This present moment is the best place you can work.

Saint Germain used the I AM words to manifest.

Why not start right here and now, and choose *even more joy* in your life? How do you choose more joy?

Example: Think about the nice things in your life for which you can be grateful. Go within and feel thankful, show your gratitude. Think of all the little and big things that are right about you, your life, and how happy you are about being alive and experiencing life. Think about how connected you are to God and that He, She or It (The Source) has it all worked out for your benefit. There can't be a mistake! Everything is happening on purpose and for my greater good. I can't help having experiences that I enjoy. Life is full of good times.

The Law of Visualization

Now you may want to take even greater control over your destiny by using the outline below:

1.   Picture the outcome you want.

2.   Visualize it with feeling, use "your" imagination, noticing the color. Make the color more vibrant. See the detail, texture, sound, brightness, or dullness. Make it brighter and bigger. Is it close up to you or far off? Make it bigger and close up. Does it have a border? Visualize until it feels more real to you. Does your dream object have sound? If so, make it better. It is moving closer and closer to you, becoming more real. It is entering your energy field. It is lighting up your life.

3.   See it as finished. See happy faces and smiles.

4.   Open your heart to receive.

5. Show gratitude, feel worthy, feel deserving, and feel you have earned it.

6. Celebrate. Look for reasons to celebrate.

7. Be happy. Look for reasons to be happy.

8. Say, "Thank You, God, for helping me see and understand that You have already finished my project for me."

How many times do you give thanks for what you have? Not enough, I'm sure. It is the fuel that pumps the fountain of wealth and abundance. Look for synchronicity in life and celebrate.

Another of the secrets is learning how to guide your mind to create your desire.

How often have you noticed that you actually created an abundance for yourself? This could be an abundance of pain, misery, fear, pop cans, pencils, lovers, junk cars, newspapers, old magazines, bills, teaspoons, money, love, respect, babies, people offering advice, dust, rust, birds, cats, etc. You are the creator. It's all in your mind. If you don't like the results of your creation, guide your mind to create what you want instead of letting it run amok. The result, whether you like it or not, shows how your creative force is focused.

CONTRAST AND CONFLICT ARE NOT BAD

Contrast is good for you. Contrast lets you know what you don't want. It motivates you to make choices. It usually gets you off your butt when nothing else will. Contrasts are part of this universe. Hot and cold, weak and strong, on and off, like or dislike, sick or healthy, poor or rich, thick or thin encourage experiences, and somewhere in between is usually your comfort zone.

A contrast might be my missing my airplane. I did not like it at the time. I would have chosen to arrive at the airport on the correct day, not a day late. It turned out for the best that I missed the plane. I had a chance to practice manifesting and was challenged at every moment to *feel bad or look for the blessing.* The actual day of my scheduled flight I spent with my son.

When my son was 4 ½ years old, the friendly doctor next door that we trusted as a friend gave Tony Ritalin. That drug turned him into a boy with lifetime schizophrenia. His normal life has been ruined now for 59 years.

Drugs are poisonous no matter where you get them. It makes little difference whether it is from a store or the street!

He's been in and out of mental hospitals most of his adult life. I was able to take him out of the care facility, and we spent most of the day scooter riding all over Panama City. We had a great time together. On one hand, I want to do all the "correct" things and on the other hand I go with the "flow." I treasure the day Tony and I spent together. Many times, he has mental problems or seems over medicated. Having that extra day made available by missing the plane was a blessing.

Go with the flow — meaning be open to benefits from everything life offers you even the contrasts.

Welcoming contrasts with openness are desirable but not easy to do. Do you prefer to get the maximum experience from life? If so, be open to flow with what is coming down the road. Our hardships are blessings in disguise.

Having contrasts in our lives, goes well with our mental equipment. We have a comparison computer in the brain. The brain likes to make judgments and sort experiences by categories and feelings-good or bad, beneficial, or a waste of time. It is always judging. It has a left and right side. The right side is metaphysical and intuitive while the left side is logical and mathematical. When you choose not to judge, guess what side of the brain you are using? The right side, the spiritual side. Spiritual experiences are the ones that bring you inner joy. They are something that money can't buy.

By making judgments we affect our energy fields. That's why the old books say, "Judge not!"

CHANGES YOU CHOOSE TO MAKE IN YOUR LIFE.

List 10 changes:

1.

2.

3.

4.

5.

6.

7.

8.

9.

10.

11. I will stay off drugs (street or prescribed) and help my body heal as nature intended.

OTHER HIDDEN SECRETS!
MORE HIDDEN INFORMATION

How about learning the secrets to good health? Which of the following add to a longer, healthier life? Is it vitamins and minerals, amino acids, vegetables, acupressure, energy work, Reiki energy training, exercise, diet, family genes, regular checkups, positive thoughts, stress-free living, a secret procedure, or just avoiding junk food, food additives, fried foods, sugars, artificial foods, margarine, corn oil, canola oil, soybean, homogenized milk, and preservatives. How to tell the correct route through the labyrinth for you?

The next chapter introduces muscle testing. Muscle testing is allowing the Life Manager to talk to you and answer yes or no to questions having to do with what is good for the body, etc. The subconscious mind is a powerhouse for manifesting when used in the correct manner.

Muscle testing connects the conscious mind with the subconscious mind via the Life Manager.

With these questions answered, you actually know what food is good for you.

You can also ask it to tell you on a scale of 1 to 10 where you are in your ability to allow money and other wealth to flow into your life.

This kind of information makes it possible to make changes from a place of knowing rather than guessing.

8

YOUR SUBCONSCIOUS MIND AND THE LIFE MANAGER

HOW TO COMMUNICATE AND ALLOW THEM TO BE YOUR BEST FRIENDS

HOW TO USE THIS BUILT-IN POWERHOUSE FOR YOUR BENEFIT

GETTING TO THE MEAT

Ask: On a scale of 1 to 10 (10 being success) where am I in regard to my acquiring the success or wealth I desire?

Now you have enough information about possible reasons for your personal brand of poverty to be ready for big changes. If you have just scanned through the previous chapters to get to the punch line, I urge you to realize that there are several punch lines in each chapter. The buildup of understanding as you go along will give this chapter much more value to you. If you haven't studied Chapters 1-7, please go back now and do so.

Poverty or lack of sufficient funds is a dis-ease just like any other sickness, it is not terminal, and it may seem to be in your genetics.

Conversing with your very powerful subconscious mind via the Life Manager can help you find the root cause of the sickness called poverty as it relates to your life.

How do we converse with the Life Manager (LM)?

Through the yes or no answers that you receive when you ask questions in these four ways:

1.   Silently (asking silent questions).

2.   Out loud (is better).

3.   Write the question out on a piece of paper (the best). When you have a clear written question, then it's best to read it out loud to the Life Manager (LM).

4.   Or you could ask another person who is better trained in muscle testing to help you find the answers.

You might ask the LM if you have suffered a loss in a past life because you had great wealth.

You will receive answers from the Life Manager. You can get percentages, using a 1 to 10 scale. You can find out dates when a problem started, numbers of years ago your poverty really started, etc. (you may find it started years before you were born). We receive these answers through muscle testing.

The LM may keep money away from you because it wants to protect you from a perceived threat because of previous life experiences with money.

We have found that the most important requirement for healing any negative pattern is finding the root cause.

The root cause is the actual beginning event of a disorder such as poverty or dis-ease. In many cases, this primary event didn't happen during this life experience.

We have found so much evidence of previous life problems bleeding over into this current life. It matters not what you currently believe. Pretend that you have had other life experiences and work with the Life Manager to erase the problems.

The big question facing any healer is, "How do I find this starting point?" Did the issue travel to the present through the genetics? Was it inherited? Did it cross over from some other you in your Circle of Existence? (All is now! All is one!) Is it from the future? Is it from the past? Is it from a parallel universe? Is it from your childhood? From a movie or a book, you experienced and took on as your problem? The lack-of-money problem could be based on something you heard your parents say when you were a small child.

The part of you that has the knowledge about these events is your subconscious mind (SCM). It can answer all these questions when you develop a way to communicate with it.

Although it is known as the subconscious mind there is nothing sub about it. It is a very important component of your being. It knows everything about you, everything ever done to you, everything you've ever thought or felt about what happened to you, and everything you've ever done to others. These feelings and situations are stored there and affect your current now.

Inner thoughts, feelings, and expectations dictate what your outer reality will be like.

THE LIFE MANAGER IS ALWAYS WITH YOU...

Know you are not alone, because the Life Manager is always with you. The Life Manager is part of all subconscious minds and does everything it can to bring all of your desires to you.

How does it know what you want? It always notices your self-talk. Have you ever listened to your own self- talk or to the self-talk of others? If you listen, you'll quickly see why your life is the way it is.

Your outer reality is reflected by your inner self-talk!

How would you like to consciously work with the Life Manager giving it the information on exactly what you want? You can tell it to bring you even more joy, love, and abundance.

The three parts of the mind you need to understand are:
1. Conscious
2. Subconscious
3. Superconscious

The Life Manager is a subdivision of the subconscious mind.

THE SUBCONSCIOUS MIND IS LIKE A HUGE CORPORATION

This very large corporation-like-presence extends into several dimensions and contains past-life experiences and well as the future. The Life Manager division is right here with you-it is your local branch office! It is constantly sending messages so you can meet the right people to bring your desires to life. How would you like to learn how to communicate better messages and, therefore, receive better results from life? Does this sound good?

The third part of the mind is the superconscious mind. It is the consciousness version of the Internet. The Life Manager also places ads on the Net for things you want in the future. You'll want to take notice of the types of ads you are placing in the *inner Internet classified section.* Your ads may need deleting or modifying if you want to achieve the success you desire. Are you getting the life you want? Are you sometimes frustrated with what life is bringing to your table?

The root cause of poverty can be healed!
(Somewhere or somehow, you are pushing away
success.)

You only need to find out where those thoughts are
hiding.

This same, so-called, subconscious mind has been with you in all the existences (other lives, too) you've ever had or ever will have. I personally believe we are taught that it is sub so we won 't realize how important it is to us.

Perhaps the most important exercise you'll ever practice is communication with the Life Manager part of the subconscious mind.

Communication with the Life Manager is best if it is two-way instead of just constantly asking for things or writing wish lists.

MUSCLE TESTING

"TWO-WAY CONVERSATIONS"

We've adopted muscle testing as a tool for communicating with the SCM. It's a simple mechanical/electrical process that will do the job until a better one comes along. It's based on tiny electrical impulses from the brain being sent to an indicator muscle to give a positive or negative signal to the physical body. Intuition is one of our other natural abilities to know things without direct knowledge. It may kick in sometimes and give us a direct answer.

You can muscle test like the chiropractors discovered in the 30s. They tested to see if a particular adjustment made the patient's arm stronger or weaker. This now ancient method requires two people to test. We've found that one person can muscle test using the fingers of both hands. You take the thumb and forefinger of each hand and link them together. Like two links of a chain. You hold both sets of thumb and forefinger tips tightly together so you can't pull them apart with a heavy, steady pull.

When conversing with the Life Manager, it's good to ask if it will answer your questions.

Next, you introduce yourself to the Life Manager. You explain that you're becoming aware, and that you'd like to ask it some questions. Ask it to answer your questions by holding your thumb and forefinger tightly together for a "yes" and by relaxing one set and allow them to slip through the other for a "no."

Most people can do this immediately with varying degrees of confidence.

Occasionally, we have a student who has been killed or tortured for doing healing work in several of their former lives. If this is the case, the Life Manager may think that this kind of activity could lead to death and will be reluctant to allow you to participate in muscle testing. (An instructor questions the student's Life Manager and heals the energy blockages from the past life using Laser Reiki and Cosmic Energetic Healing techniques.)

Next, we convince the Life Manager that it's safe to do muscle testing. That no one is going to torture or kill their body if they do muscle testing, because times have changed. The best way to convince the Life Manager is to heal the root cause event that caused it to judge the practice of muscle testing and healing to be a dangerous activity. This was one of our first lessons in muscle testing when we were noticing that Roi's fingers didn't want to work correctly.

If one of us can do this, we all can.

Is that because we are all One?

ROI'S PERSONAL CHALLENGE WITH MUSCLE TESTING

Roi comments: "When we discovered that individuals could do muscle testing by themselves (using just their thumb and fingers), we found that Taylore could do it and I could not. The Life Manager was refusing to allow me to do individual muscle testing. I was wondering why I couldn't, and she could?

"We all know that if one human (male or female) can do something, all others are hard-wired for it, too. That had been proven to us in our fire walking experiences. Our bodies are equipped to protect themselves if we can convince them that it's necessary. That is why fire walking works.

"Obviously the subconscious mind had been convinced that communicating with me in the physical would be hazardous to my body's health. It was protecting me from something! But what?

"We tried another approach!

"Taylore could use her thumb and forefinger linked to a set of mine. Hers would answer the questions, but mine wouldn't. We both asked questions about the root cause of my fingers not wanting to react, and soon discovered the reason. The questions were: 'Was it dangerous for me to muscle test?' 'Yes!' 'Is it your belief that something bad might happen to me if I am allowed to do this?' 'Yes!' 'Did something happen to me in the past?' 'Yes!' 'Does it have anything to do with healing others?' 'Yes!' 'Can this condition be corrected?' 'Yes!' 'Will you show us the root cause?' 'Yes!'

"We asked many yes and no questions about what might have happened in the past. Finally, we asked if I had been punished for healing others. We got a strong 'Yes!' We found that I had been tortured, punished, and even killed many times for showing healing powers and/or teaching others. 'Can this be healed so I can muscle test?' 'Yes!'

"We pulled those old junk software programs out of my consciousness and re-energized my body with affirmations, such as,

> ➢ *It is now safe to do healing work!*
> ➢ *It is good to teach others to heal!*
> ➢ *I like being able to communicate with the Life Manager!*

"Many of our students have similar problems. They also had been punished for healing and/or showing their spiritual powers in their past lives. My experience has taught us how to overcome these problems. All of our students can now communicate with their subconscious minds! Thank You, God, for having helped us make this communications breakthrough!"

End of Roi 's personal challenge. Roi is now a master teacher of muscle testing.

MUSCLE TESTING IS USUALLY CALLED APPLIED KINESIOLOGY

As defined by the Kinesiology Federation in Great Britain: "Kinesiology literally means the study of body movement; it is a holistic approach to balancing the movements and interaction of a person's energy systems. Gentle assessment of muscle response monitors (those areas) where blocks and imbalances are impairing physical, emotional, or energetic well-being."

You can learn how to reliably converse with the subconscious mind and the Life Manager.

• A formal introduction to the Life Manager establishes a direct line of communication.

• You will learn to receive a simple "yes" or "no" answer to direct questions to the Life Manager through muscle testing. You 'll even be able to detect a "maybe" or determine if the question should be restated.

• You will learn how to reverse the question to double-check your answers.

When you take our seminars, you will refine this mode of interrogation to determine and clear the root cause(s) of countless dis-eases, problems, and learning situations in the physical, mental, emotional, and spiritual arenas of life.

You can also get help through an inexpensive phone consultation. See information on our website.

THE FORMAL INTRODUCTION

Set the stage with your subconscious mind. Tell it who you are and that you want to access the Life Manager through muscle testing. Explain that this is not a test of will or strength but a way of talking to your body. The body will tell you yes or no by either locking (yes) or unlocking (no) the muscles tested. After you ask the LM to hold tight, allow 2 seconds to give the body a chance to react accordingly. Practice with simple questions. Is this an apple? Is that an orange? Then switch the items and ask again. Allow your connection with the LM to grow. Use it to test what foods are good for you. Canola oil vs. olive oil, sugar vs. a piece of fruit, etc. Soon you will develop confidence in asking questions and receiving the answers. The LM knows how many vitamin pills will do you the most good or if this is the correct brand for you, and how many times a day you should take them.

The following exercise is for two people, one testing the other (using the arm as an indicator lever.)

You may have seen two people testing bottles of vitamins in a health food store by testing the arm strength.

Hi, Life Manager, I'm Taylore. I'm the one in the body who's becoming aware, and I'd like to work with you in clearing some issues. Is that okay with you?

1. Apply a light, steady pressure on the arm being tested. Avoid quick jerky movements. Ease the pressure on and off. Use a proper leverage point on the arm according to the strength needed to test.

2. Explain what is a "yes" and what is a "no." Holding the arm muscles tight is a "yes," while releasing the muscles and weakening the arm is a "no."

3. Next, ask the LM to show you a "yes." Ask it to show you a "no." The arm should be strong for a "yes" and weak for a "no."

4. If you ask the person if their name is: (use their actual name), the arm will say "yes". Then ask them if their name is John Wayne or Jane Doe or if they are currently a green frog? Their muscles will unlock and say "no."

5. Now you have established a communication link with the body and the Life Manager. You will begin to have confidence in your ability.

There are many ways to refine muscle/kinesiology testing.

We teach several ways in our workshops. Through our 14 years of experience, we both have found it is easier and quicker to just use our own fingers to muscle test for the individual. This is a requirement for remote healing because you don't have the client's arms for testing. When using your own hands and fingers for testing someone else, you need to connect with their subconscious mind to find the negative patterns to release. You never do any testing or healings without their permission. Time, space, and distance are no barrier to instant communication.

Kinesiology — a form of communication with the body's own intelligence, has been around under the same name since the 1930's.

When doing muscle testing, the wisdom is always in the question.

When you are learning to use muscle testing, we suggest that you write each question down. Rewrite your question, refining it until it is straight forward without any ambiguities and can be answered with a yes, no, number, or percentage.

Jane Holdway's Kinesiology, Muscle Testing and Energy Balancing for Health and Well-Being states: "The body is all one interacting unit, an intrinsic whole with many different parts, systems, and functions which interconnect and affect each other. Some of the things we do can cause an imbalance in our bodies. The body often sends out warning signals that all is not well, aches and pains, minor digestion upsets, generally feeling tired, tension, lack of concentration, crying for no apparent reason and so on. Unfortunately, we don't always heed these warnings and often wait until the body starts to break down before taking any action."

NOTE: The subconscious mind does not hear or take notice of the words no, or I don 't want, etc.

For example, your friend says, "I 'm never going to get married again." What does your friend do? The next thing you know they are married. Why? The SCM does not understand **no** or never, so it hears I am going to get married again from his never statement.

Why just settle and "get by" when you know you deserve abundance.

What about the words no fear! This is a command to fear. We're always giving mixed messages to children. We tell them, "Don't fall!" What are we really commanding them to do? To fall! It is no surprise that sooner or later they fall. We tell them to not get dirty. What do they do? Get dirty. I wonder why we aren't taught these simple truths at an early age. I wonder what it would be like *to grow up without all these negative mind programs put in our consciousness by well-meaning parents.*

I remember from when I was about three or four years old, my mother asked me to go to the garden and hoe the peas. I didn't miss a one!

She didn't tell me to hoe the weeds from around the peas. The Life Manager will answer the exact question you ask, so be precise.

What you resist persists!

What you fight against pulls you into it!

NOTE: Never use the word need in your requests. Need is a "get by" or begging word.

DOES "SAY NO TO DRUGS" WORK?

Of course, it does! Drug use picked up tremendously because of that slogan. *Oops!* (Or was that the hidden plan all along?)

Does war lead to peace?

Drug use picked up considerably with the inception of the nationwide campaign called DARE. These are three of the things causing an increase in drug use.

Love leads to love.

War leads to war.

1. The extra emphasis on formal education of the different kinds of drugs they are not to use created the energy and interest to go out and experiment with drugs.

• *Where our attention goes, so does our mind.* The more you know about anything, the more it's embedded into your energy field. The more you fight against something, the more you are sucked into its energy.

With muscle testing you can test to see if D.A.R.E. has in mind the highest good for all concerned.

• Remember the TV preachers who preached and fought against sin, prostitution, and greed? It was a shock to most people when they became personally involved in doing exactly what they were fighting against. Think about this.

• Human nature. When I was a kid, I'd do anything someone *dared* me to do or not to do. Kids go through this. Thank God, we don't stay there for long.

• By saying *no to drugs,* what is the real message they are giving to the SCM? What are the kids going to do? They are going to take drugs. (Remember the subconscious mind doesn't hear the word no.)

Do you suppose that someone behind the scenes who designed this campaign knew it would increase drug use?

PULLING OUT THE ROOT CAUSE

Using muscle testing, go down your list of questions, looking for the cause of one of your particular energy blockages (a reoccurring pattern of energy) that is keeping money and success away from you. Take notes. Once you find the root cause event, pull it out of your consciousness by making a sweeping motion with your hand down and out, away from your body.

Here are some suggestions for questions. Most people have some of these anti-wealth patterns plugging up their abundance.

1. Money is the root of all evil.

2. You must have a good formal education before you can succeed.

3. You must work hard and long.

4. It is dangerous to have lots of money.

5. There are inner self-sabotaging programs of:
   • Unworthiness
   • Not good enough
   • Not approving of self
   • Not loving self

6. Money is bad.

7. It is easy for others but hard for you.

8. You'll never be well off, affluent, etc.

9. _____

10. _____

11. _____

12. _____

Have you ever in all these thousands of years taken a vow of poverty?

Has it ever been removed?

Go down your list, testing each to see if any of those negative patterns of lack are present in your energy field. You will need to find a yes or no answer for each question. Pull the problem out of your energy field as explained above.

Anti-wealth programs are software to your mind and push success away from you.

Now that you've taken something out of your energy field, you have to put something back.

Breathe in these words: "Peace, love joy, and abundance for the best and highest good for all concerned." Feel the new energy frequency move throughout your body. Also breathe in: "I accept even more prosperity, wealth and abundance." Feel it in your body as you breathe it in!

Connect with any book. Ask the Life Manager to go out to the universe and ask what percentage of truth a certain book contains.

After you have done all the muscle-testing exercises several times and/or gotten a friend to help you who does it easily, if it still isn't dependable for you, it would be a good idea to come to a workshop, receive telephone coaching, or arrange for a remote healing. Details can be found in the appendix.

A recent 20-year study on using the SCM to retrieve all sorts of valuable information is cited in the book *Power Vs. Force* by David Hawkins, MD. This is, by far, the most complete authority on muscle testing.

We discovered this book after we'd been using muscle-testing methods to identify and remove negative energy patterns in our healing practices. We noticed that Dr. Hawkins apparently didn't know about one person doing muscle-testing by himself, but we got other valuable ideas from his book. In later editions, he does give information on personal self-muscle testing.

LOOKING DOWN WHILE MUSCLE TESTING

Looking down accesses the kinesthetic modality of the body where the sensation of presence, movement, and stimulations of sensory nerve endings in muscles, tendons, and joints are more noticeable.

When asking the SCM questions, it is good to look slightly down to improve the access to answers. Remember, we are looking for slight changes in the muscles, either a tightening or loosening of the indicator.

Sometimes the body will switch, and your fingers pull apart for Yes and stay together for No. To reestablish the correct answers, it may be necessary to ask the Life Manager to "show me what a Yes is... and what a No is." You simply re-ask the Life Manager to have your fingers hold together for a Yes, etc.

FINE TUNING

You might ask it to intensify the feelings or movements, so the correct answer is more easily identified.

We know how vital this chapter is to you and to your ability to get a clear picture of where your recurring blockages are stored. In order to receive all the abundance and wealth that is due to you, you can learn to use the Life Manager division of the SCM to find and clear any obstacles on your path (no matter what your karma is or what others have told you).

A person could have told you, "You'll never be rich," and that becomes a huge obstacle. We know you can overcome any negative thought pattern and become as wealthy as you desire. If you need extra help, see our Appendix for workshops, counseling, and healing services offered.

Obstacles I've overcome:

Obstacles I'm working on:

9

DOGMAS EAT YOUR WEALTH

THE LAST OBSTACLE TO OVERCOME BEFORE YOU RECEIVE YOUR PROSPERITY

DOGMAS ARE BLOCKAGES THAT NEED TO BE RELEASED

Dogmas are simple phrases that have been repeated to us as facts. They've been repeated frequently, some of them for thousands of years. They weren't true then, and they still aren't true. They cannot be proven as facts, but the mind treats them as if they are real. Dogmas must be ferreted out, examined, uninstalled, erased, abolished, overridden, overwritten, etc.

Example: "Money is the root of all evil." Actually, money is simply energy stored from labor of some kind.

Another group of junk software in our mind (the body's computer like brain) is dogmas.

DOGMAS MAKE YOU THINK YOU HAVE TO LIVE UP TO THEM-OR DOWN TO THEM-AS IF THEY WERE TRUE

What are dogmas? Unproven ideas or beliefs that you've bought into existence without firsthand experience. Holding them in place takes up a lot of your energy. According to the dictionary, "dogmas are religious beliefs authorities consider to be absolute truths." You also have dogmas that aren't religious beliefs. What do they do for you? Nothing good! They block your creativity. Dogmas are energy blockages and should be released from your energy field. They give mixed messages to the subconscious mind (SCM). Some dogmas can come in on the genetics from our parents and grandparents.

MOST PEOPLE HAVE NO IDEA OF THE ONGOING DAMAGE THAT DOGMAS DO

You consume a lot of your creative energy holding dogmas in place.

Every creative idea, every thought you think gets filtered through a platter full of your dogmas before your conscious mind gets to see it. Your particular set of dogmas is like a series of filters that strains your thoughts to make them conform. It is very hard for new thoughts or new ideas to come to you. It takes a lot of energy to hold these false beliefs in place. They no longer serve you, probably have never served you, and may have been in place from other lifetimes.

In my studies of energy blockages, I have found that you can release a huge burden from your energy field by releasing dogmas that no longer serve you.

Do you believe in past lives? If so, how are your vows and beliefs from other lives affecting you now?

Have the dogmas been uninstalled, deleted, gotten rid of?

Here is a partial list of dogmas & vows that tie up much of your energy:

vows of poverty
cultural dogmas (all kinds)
race dogmas (that one race is better than another, etc.)
social consciousness dogmas
the need to conform
the need to be liked
the need to fit in
the need to control
the need to judge
sexual dogmas
vows of chastity
vows of marriage
vows of loyalty to spouses
belief in the need to grow old
belief in the need to look old
the need for punishment
the need to fix everything
the need to fix everybody
religious dogmas
brand of religions
ancient religions
the original sin
vows of humility
vows of obedience
the Ten Commandments and hundreds of other commandments (are still operating behind the scenes, whether you think you believe in them or not.)

MONEY DOGMAS AND OLD SAYINGS:

There are hundreds of money dogmas. They sure don't serve you. Chase them out of your energy field.

vows of poverty
money is bad-it is not spiritual
I always have bad luck
you have to work hard to get ahead
*a rich man can't get into heaven any more than a camel can get through the eye of the needle **
no pain- no gain
the rich get richer while the poor get poorer
you can't get something from nothing
you can't take it with you
if I'm a good person, I'll give all my money away and take care of others
easy come- easy go
not valuing what comes easily or without effort or cost
you can have nothing good without sacrifice, suffering, and struggle

* Incidentally "the eye of the needle" in those days referred to the entrances to walled cities. The doors were purposely made low so a band of marauders on camels couldn't gallop into the city. The camel couldn't even crawl on its knees and fit through the door, so the city was easier to defend.

I release the need for hard lessons.

I am learning from lessons that come easy.

You can muscle test: How many times have you vowed to be loyal to one person forever?

Is that a conflict in your mind, or not?

YOU HAVE NO NEED TO WORRY:

DOGMAS ARE EASY TO GET RID OF

Even if you don't believe in them, they can get stuck in your energy field and cause problems of lack and confusion about being able to accept success. If your energy field is full of poverty programs (dogmas) then where can you put success programs?

How many vows of poverty have you taken?

Obviously, this is a huge one to clear if wealth and happiness are on your wish list.

This is one reason that all the self-improvements work you have done has gotten you very little progress.

You might be curious about how and why dogmas get started. Any time a dogma comes to your attention, examine it closely to see if belief in it would benefit some particular group. Money dogmas obviously benefit the wealthy. Here's an example that must have been invented by a rich person: "The rich get richer, and the poor get poorer." I can see them laughing all the way to the bank! From their ongoing experiences, however, the wealthy know that those money dogmas are definitely not to be taken seriously by themselves, such as this one, "If you're wealthy, you're not a good person."

The way to rid yourself of dogmas is to state the words or phrase of the dogma and say "Release!" as you make a sweeping down and away motion with your hand. After I do this energy clearing for clients, I notice a remarkable increase in their energy. They report feeling much lighter, brighter, and better able to handle their lives.

The energy it takes to hold these false beliefs in place is released. It is now available to help return the body to health, wellbeing, and affluence. When you finish sweeping away the dogmas, breathe in beautiful bright, golden light and feel it healing your body, mind, and spirit. Feel your body becoming lighter.

Once again: The simplest method for clearing a dogma or belief from your energy field is to state the dogma and brush it out of your body's energy field. It also helps tremendously to align your polarities with the Earth and the cosmos, as taught earlier in this book, before and after releasing each dogma or negative belief.

Have you ever taken a vow of chastity?

Do you have a hard time getting or staying married?

Sometimes a particularly strong belief about yourself or about a certain cultural rule you adhere to might take a few weeks to clear completely. Do not get frustrated. These recurring patterns of lack, limitation, and poverty are coming out of your body, and you'll feel lighter. You're setting yourself free to think instead of being dictated to by your old destructive belief patterns. Be happy that the dogmas are leaving and rejoice that you've found yet another one to release. Sometimes there are layers upon layers, and only time and persistence will clear them.

Since we are making a big deal about this, maybe we should give you another reason why you might want to rid yourself of outdated beliefs, vows, and dogmas. I'm sure a good imaginative mind like yours could ferret out hundreds of reasons. For instance, vows of marriage are sometimes stated as if forever. What if down through the ages 100 of your marriage vows were stated with great emotion as forever? And now here you are, inside a good and loving marriage with some little conflicting thoughts in your head.

Remember, your subconscious mind takes everything literally. So deep down, the Life Manager is considering you to be a liar, untrustworthy, an adulterer, and a scam artist because of all the other vows stored in the archives. Dump the conflicting programs and your relationships will grow and bloom.

PUT NEW EMPOWERING BELIEFS INTO THE BODY/MIND FIELD

All right! So, you've begun releasing old beliefs-one at a time. It's now time to put new ones in one at a time.

165

"I release the dogma of _____ and all the pain, struggle, guilt, frustration, sadness, anger, and suffering caused by it. I also release the memory and the habit of it. I am now completely free and clear of all this _____ dogma."

Give yourself a pat on the back! You are well on your way to freedom and wealth!

And then:

"I embrace and accept the abundant gifts of the universe with gratitude, love, and joy.

"I joyfully and expectantly am open to receive even more wealth, harmony and balance to continually flow into my life.

"Thank You, God, (Source, etc.) for even more money, joy and freedom!

So be it, and so it is!

10

THE SEVEN PRINCIPLES FOR CREATING YOUR PROSPERITY

1. Recognize the role of self-talk, mind chatter, and automatic responses in receiving or blocking wealth.

2. Embrace the power of your subconscious mind and the way it works for you. You can use it to find and delete unproductive mind programs and other mental and emotional junk software.

3. One of the greatest powers is the power to choose your thoughts and how you will act rather than just reacting to outer circumstances.

4. The power of writing down your desires in a positive manner and then reading the list to the Life Manager. The power is derived from natural laws.

5. The power inherent in mental fasting from negative thoughts, plus training the mind to focus only on positive thoughts. The power to focus

your thoughts only on things you really want to have in your life experiences. Focus on your destination and not on how you will get there.

6. Use the Laws:
    a) The Law of Attraction
    b) The Law of Allowance
    c) The Law of Gratitude

7. Embrace the essence of

• loving who you are
• loving what you are
• loving where you are
• loving what you have

Meditate on these before you try to move beyond.

11

LIVE ON THE PLAY AS YOU GO PLAN

This last chapter is an addition we made to this manual when we realized we had not even mentioned how important it is to have fun throughout your life rather than save it all up for your retirement. To illustrate what an important component of your life that is I need to give you a little more of my background.

I first got married when I was 18 years old and my bride, Rosemary, was 17. It seems like we almost immediately had 3 small children but that didn't stop us from living on the play as you go plan.

I had a motorcycle because I had been working at an Indian motorcycle shop, so we rode the bike and explored all the back roads in that area of central Ohio.

Motorcycle shops barely made it in those days, before Honda, so to get the extra money we needed for a growing family, I took a job doing the service and most of the sales for a Crosley garage.

Next, I was working for a White Truck dealer but all the time we kept doing fun stuff and we started our first tiny business on the side. You notice I didn't say "small business" because most people think it is a small business when you only hire 8 to 10 people.

We did this business ourselves and it wasn't long before we were making enough on the side for me to quit my day job and devote full time to this much more fun tiny business of selling speed equipment and modifying cars.

Still, on the play as you go plan, we decided to sell most of our stuff and move to Oregon because Rosemary's mom and stepfather had moved to Medford about 5 years before and kept telling us how great it was.

In Oregon, I worked at assembling farm equipment, and we explored all over southern Oregon in our spare time.

We started another tiny business repairing cars and bought a small trailer to live in that we could easily pull with our Chevy van.

Soon, we found a service station that had an empty service bay for our car repair business, and we were able to park our trailer next to it. No more trailer park rent and a real place of business at a reasonable rate.

We developed a pretty good business with a lot of repeat customers. After we had been there for about a year, one of our customers told us how he went to Boise, Idaho to ride motorcycles on the hundreds of miles of open trails above Boise. He explained that you could ride your dirt bike right from your house to open trails that started right at the edge of the town.

Since we lived on the play as you go plan and that sounded like a fun place to live, we gave the station owner notice and a month or so later, we moved our trailer to Boise, Idaho.

Boise was a pretty nice little town back in the 1950s and we had probably been there a couple of days when I saw a mechanic wanted sign in an automotive shop, so we checked it out. It was a transmission shop run by a guy named Felix who had moved to Boise from Rock Springs, Wyoming.

The unique thing was that he didn't hire anyone to work there. You worked there for yourself and paid him a percentage of each job. What a neat (low paperwork) way to run a service business.

After we had been there about a year, a lady ran in to Rosemary's motorcycle and did about $800 worth of damage without hurting her. I fixed it for $200 and she bought a toy she had been wanting for $100.00 and we had $500.00 left over, so we went into the motorcycle business part time.

Within a short time, too many people were coming to the transmission shop to talk motorcycles and Felix said I should either concentrate on transmissions or go open a motorcycle shop.

We rented an old flower shop in Garden City, which is on the other side of the river from most of Boise and were able to park our now much bigger trailer behind it. That $500.00 invested in our tiny business and of course work and promotion bought us 2 trips to Japan, a vacation in Hawaii, and 3 trips to Europe, and allowed us to live on the play as you go plan for about 20 years.

As it turned out, if we had been waiting for our retirement to have fun, Rosemary would have been cheated big time because she was diagnosed with cancer at the age of 38.

The doctors and hospital managed to kill her in about a year with their so-called treatments. They used poisonous (chemotherapy) and radiation (also a poison) on her because we didn't know any better at the time. (You cannot poison someone back to health.)

My sons and I sold the business a couple of years later and the property alone that the business had paid for brought us close to $100,000.00, all from that $500.00 left over from Rosemary's accident.

Taylore and I are currently enjoying the proceeds of a $500.00 tiny business we started together in 1990. So far, it has supported us from shortly after its start and has made the payments on our 23-acre Reiki Ranch and much more and the end of this tiny business is not in sight.

Retirement? Why would we want to stop doing what we love to sit on the couch, watch TV, and eat chips, when it is so much more fun to follow these several tiny businesses, we've built from that $500.00 investment in us and see where they end up.

The point is a fun play as you go jobless life is just as available to any of you as it is to us.

This tiny $500.00 business built up faster and bigger than the first one did because we had discovered the power of "even more" just before we started this one, and we use even more constantly.

There is no limit to what you can do also just by using the mental technology we have gifted to you in this book.

By the way, we have benefitted greatly from what we learned from Felix and have never hired any employees to work in our various tiny businesses, we have always used contract labor, just like he did.

Always minimize your paperwork because the usual paperwork never makes you money, and it's more fun to be around people who can think for themselves.

Are you beginning to see that real success in your life and business success has to include fun?

We always have lived on the "play as you go plan" and it has served us well.

To start and build a substantial business on a tiny amount of money, you certainly don't pay yourself a salary and make payments on a bunch of toys. No payments, unless it is necessary for the business, is a good habit to cultivate and certainly no expensive clothes and meals until your tiny amount of money has multiplied several times.

About the only time I had a job was while I was saving money to start a business, and if I had any payments, they just made me have to have a job longer.

If you are worth hiring, you can at a minimum, make twice the money doing something similar in your own tiny business. But you might think, "I have no business experience or training in accounting, etc."

Just keep it simple and count your money. If you spend more than you receive you are not doing it right, so pay attention and correct it.

It is not rocket science, it's simply the stuff they don't teach you in school because they are training you to be a big spending wage slave.

Just do something on your own in your free time and upset their plans.

It usually doesn't take too long before you are making more in your spare time than you are being paid at the job, and that may mean it's time to become creatively jobless.

That's exactly what I have done several times. They were not all big winners but most of them paid their way and without doing them I would not have gained the necessary experience to make it big with my two $500.00 winners.

In earlier chapters, we have helped you get the proper mind set to do the same as we have.

Really spend some time understanding the simplicity we've given you to work with:

You too can be a jobless winner in life and have the fun of making it big while you hang out here in the third dimension.

Roi

APPENDIX

You have just studied the do-it-yourself manual (The Joy of Being Jobless). It has given you several simple actions you can take to increase your affluence and erase your personal poverty consciousness.

> Those who've made these simple changes have as much as tripled their income without working any harder or getting more formal education. The subtitle How to Obtain Financial Freedom applies here and can be applied to your life as well.

This manual was written 10 years after Laser Reiki was discovered, but it was always cooking on the back burner. We realized that people needed a prosperity study guide to help them understand that their lack of wealth can be healed just like any other sickness. In our energy healing school hundreds of students and clients have improved their health and finances by eliminating energy blockages. Keeping good health and attracting wealth is an ongoing process.

'Remember: You're always just a few thoughts or beliefs away from attracting the wealth and better health you've wanted. Below you will see some extra educational tools to help you succeed in all areas of your life.

Courses, Classes, Workshops, and Retreats at the Reiki Ranch - 9 miles West of I-5, near Chehalis, Washington.

Reiki I, Reiki II and Reiki III are traditional Usui Reiki training. These workshops and seminars are given at least twice a year.

Reiki is the universal life force energy (God energy) that flows out the hands of a practitioner. It flows out in an even field similar to someone sprinkling the lawn with a spray of water. The energy is applied to the entire body and also on the location of the pain. Students learn to flow 4th dimensional universal healing energy to heal themselves and others by laying-on-of-hands. Simple. Easy. Practical. Reiki is taught and practiced in nearly every country of the world.

We give a Free Reiki I - 8-hour certification workshop several times a year. It is followed by Reiki II and Reiki III for a total of only $344 including all three manuals for the Master package.

The Laser Reiki Series of Workshops, the most advanced energy training, starts with LR Levels 1-4. Basic Laser Reiki is a series of 6 weekends over 6 months. It begins on Saturday morning and finishes on Sunday at 6 pm each month and the class chooses the weekend.

As a LR graduate you'll know how to:

• Use Laser Reiki - a concentrated healing beam of energy that flows out the fingertips. You will be able to flow 6th dimensional energy directly to the energy body. (That is considered 100 times more effective than sending energy to the physical body first.)

• Learn to discover and to release the root cause of the dis-ease (what started it in the first place).

176

• Remove energy blockages causing ...pain, trauma, stress, anxiety, fear, etc., instantly and be rid of its reoccurring patterns.

• Heal dis-eases several years before they become apparent.

• Do remote healings using only the person's name and location. (The person must request a healing.)

• Heal the reasons and hidden beliefs that are holding you back from success.

• Heal yourself, your friends, your family, pets and plants.

• Most importantly, you'll learn ...how to communicate through the Life Manager-with the subconscious mind (your inner powerhouse.)

Wishing to take back control of your health? Want an easy way to heal those chronic pains that have resisted treatment for many years? Try Laser Reiki training! It is unsurpassed-there are no other healing methods that work as quickly and as easily as Laser Reiki.

Why is the Laser Reiki healing method the most sought after?

Why are other practitioners: Reiki Masters, Chi Gong practitioners, Therapeutic Touch, Response Therapy, other energy workers, massage therapists, chiropractors, nurses and other health workers taking Laser Reiki?

Many professionals are adding Laser Reiki to their healing toolbox, because there is nothing else even remotely as powerful and useful in the energy healing fields. This workshop adds a whole new dimension to whatever modality you now use.

If you've never had any alternative health training before ...there is No Problem! There's no prerequisite needed for taking Laser Reiki Level 1-4.

Other workshops after Laser Reiki:

Laser Reiki 5 -- a 3-day workshop. Laser Reiki 6 -- a 3-day workshop. Laser Reiki 7 -- a 3-day workshop. Laser Reiki 8 -- a 3-day workshop.

Other courses:

Creating Your Prosperity -- 1-day workshop Cosmopathic Success Seminars -- 2-days

Healing Services:

•   One-in person or remote healing -$100 Donation

•   To have your name placed in the group prayer box for monthly healings

•   Personal healings with three or more masters working together to clear your energy-$300

Also on the Web site: free reports, articles, and schedules.

Safe nurturing natural setting for the Reiki Ranch -- Located in Lewis County, Washington, only 9+ miles from the Interstate-5 freeway. The countryside is a mixture of dairy farms, fields, and wooded hills. It is sparsely populated. The air is fresh, it's quiet, and you can see brilliant stars at night because there are no towns nearby. The Assembly of CEH purchased these beautiful grounds-22 acres country land. There are fruit trees, a spring-fed pond, spring water, small year- around mountain stream within 40 feet of the school, meditation areas, organic gardens, greenhouse, alder and fir tree farm, etc.

There are trails on the property for hiking, horse and motorcycle riding, plus an adjoining 23 miles of trails in the woods. The grounds have been blessed by angels and other etheric masters. Just being on these sacred grounds is a healing experience.

The Assembly of CEH is a nonprofit association registered with the state of Washington. Donations of all kinds are cheerfully accepted. It's been long known: "What you give back to the Source, expecting nothing, is returned to you in some way tenfold." Taylore and Roi donate all their time to this ministry.

The mission of the Assembly of CEH is to touch the hearts of millions of people, showing them a better way to connect with inner peace, love, joy, health, abundance, and prosperity.

Mailing Address ONLY!   The Assembly of CEH (Checks and other donations to be made out to this name)

1673 S. Market #143

Chehalis, WA 98532

Tel. 360-748-4426

For extra copies of the book, The Joy of Being Jobless by Taylore Vance with Herb Roi Richards, order from Top Sellers Best Sellers (buy1a.com) and Amazon, or your favorite bookstore.

Visit the Web sites for current dates, times, Reiki Ranch location, and more information.

www.LaserReiki.com, www.ReikiRanch.com, and www.CosmicEnergeticHealing.org
E-mail: ReikiRanch@gmail.com
and/or herbbike@gmail.com

Taylore Vance and Herb Roi Richards
Founders of Laser Reiki and Cosmic Energetic Healing®

Your Creative Index:

Here's where you write down the chapter and page numbers so you can easily find again your personal points of interest.

Example:

140 - The Life Manager is always with you...

NOTES:

NOTES:

NOTES:

NOTES:

NOTES:

CONSUMER ADVICE NOTICE

This book (manual) is sold as an educational tool only. We do not claim or imply any medical benefits. If you have questions regarding health care, consult your doctor, who has a license to practice. We do not claim or imply any advice on law. If you have a question regarding law, consult a lawyer or attorney. We do not give investment advice.

Made in the USA
Columbia, SC
06 October 2024

43732762R00113